LAST LETTERS
HOME

LAST LETTERS HOME

EDITED BY

Tamasin Day-Lewis

MACMILLAN

First published 1995 by Pan Books

an imprint of Macmillan General Books
Cavaye Place London SW10 9PG
and Basingstoke

Associated companies throughout the world

ISBN 0 333 64559 6

1 3 5 7 9 8 6 4 2

A CIP catalogue record for this book is available from
the British Library

Typeset by CentraCet Limited, Cambridge
Printed by Mackays of Chatham PLC, Chatham, Kent

CONTENTS

ACKNOWLEDGEMENTS

To begin at the beginning, there would not have been a book *Last Letters Home* without ITV having first commissioned the film of the same name. Stuart Prebble, ITV's factual programme commissioner made that decision, for which I am hugely thankful. His deputy, John Blake, has no small interest in the film. *Last Letters Home* is our third film together, with luck the third of many more. There are few commissioning editors with whom I have enjoyed such a creative relationship, and none I can think of who possesses such powers as an enabler, the quality I prize above all others in a director.

Having tentatively mentioned the word 'book' to my agent David Watson, he, within seconds, had got me together with Simpson Fox's literary agent Georgina Capel, who, equally swiftly, started talking to publishers. I thank her for her speed and effectiveness, and for the fun we had while selling our wares. She it was who introduced me to Macmillan's editorial director Georgina Morley. I remember hoping she'd be the one to buy it − it's so refreshing when someone is unashamedly enthusiastic, and that she hasn't ceased to be. With such a tight deadline, she began preparing instantly for our joint nervous breakdown.

I thank researcher Laura Gavshon for finding and writing about several of the contributors, which was not something she initially thought she would be doing when she agreed to help research the film. She has made an invaluable contribution to the book.

Cameraman John Warwick, sound recordist Marc Hatch and assistant cameraman Rob Hill kept asking the questions while we were filming, and were all influential in the critical decisions that had to be taken with the interviews I was doing, which were the basis for the book as well as for the film. Our three weeks on the road together, each night in a different county – or country – under constant pressure, were made fun, happy, challenging and stimulating, in more ways than one!

I could not have completed John Dossett-Davies's story without the help of Michael Stein when I was interviewing Ellen Gerlt in Gottingen, so he deserves special thanks.

Since becoming an independent director and producer I have worked closely for five happy years now with Deborah Fox. She has been production manager, critic, friend and more. As I wrote frantically through Christmas in the West of Ireland, Deborah typed up frantically in the South of France. She has also devoted a large amount of time to helping me pursue permissions, photographs and original letters. No amount of thanks is large enough. And her criticism is of the sternest.

The book, in this case, is only as good as its contributors, who, without exception, I thank for putting up with interviews, letters, telephone calls and, in some cases, the horrors of filming! Your stories and letters have made it. It is about the exceptional people who were, or still are, part of your families.

Finally a major debt of gratitude to the Imperial War Museum. Penny Ritchie-Calder, the exhibitions director, got me started with potential contributors during my first week at the museum, and was so generous with her time and her ideas. Rod Suddaby, the keeper of the Department of Documents deserves a medal for putting up with my requests for material over a five-month period. He has been unfailingly helpful and enthusiastic about the project, and suggested contributors who have come his way and whom I would never have found otherwise. He also spent time helping to trace or contact potential contributors. Without his help, there would be no book.

Tamasin Day-Lewis
9 February 1995

INTRODUCTION

Last October I was in the middle of researching the film *Last Letters Home* for ITV when the idea of a book began to implant itself.

I had already spent several weeks poring over letters, memoirs and diaries written during the Second World War, and was beginning to find it difficult, with the clear focus of the film, to discard some of the extraordinarily powerful material that was obviously not going to fit into the film's framework. It wasn't that the *Last Letters Home* theme was too limiting, more that the range and wealth of material was on a scale I hadn't guessed existed when I started the research.

I had put advertisements into local and national newspapers, done radio interviews, and contacted myriad organizations and regiments from the Royal British Legion to the Burma Star Association, in a comprehensive trawl for material and, perhaps more importantly, for people who were still alive to talk about the letters they had sent and received.

The biggest job, and the largest number of jewels, however, began to glister one morning in the Imperial War Museum's Reading Room. To say I became a regular reader there is an understatement. There were times when a sleeping bag would have been more helpful than my notebook and pen. The subject headings on each index were enormous. There was everything from Love, Romance, Death, Evacuees, Escape and Evasion, to Sex, Morals and Philosophy. Calling up the letters, I was sometimes surprised by a single gem, or a short series of letters leading up to, at best, a reunion or, at worst, death; but in many more cases there were literally hundreds of letters, often written in spider-like scrawl on faded airmail paper.

Even looking for last letters, I felt I had to read the whole collection to build up a sense of the background, the characters, circumstances, daily lives, hopes and fears, before then starting the process of trying to trace the writer or the recipient. What amazed me initially was both the quality of the letters and the extraordinary detail with which the writers relayed their daily lives, filling in all the minutiae that would have been discussed with the loved one were they to have come home every night. It wasn't always the big themes that moved me: the keeping in touch with the trivia of everyday existence in exceptional circumstances and the capacity for strength, reassurance and hope were both illuminating and humbling.

While researching and then interviewing the contributors for the film and the book, I have gradually found myself taking for granted the laws and precepts that became the *modus vivendi* of the writers and their loved ones.

Many of the people who lived through the Second World War describe it as the most exciting and dynamic period of their lives. Despite the danger, death, uncertainty and separation, it was a time when rules were broken, life was exhilarating. One contributor speaks of his first love in words that are both personal and universal, 'War is a powerful aphrodisiac.' No one knew what was going to happen to them. People lived intensely, death became commonplace for the old and the young. Another contributor remembers all her schoolfriends and forces friends just not being there at the end of the war. They had all died. Romance was quickly kindled: there was an urgency to get engaged, to marry, to have a child, perhaps to leave something behind if the couple had realistically faced up to the chances of survival, and truly accepted the uncertainty.

More poignantly, there was a sense, with so many of the men who had joined up being so young, of wanting desperately to have someone to love, to be able to write about their feelings of love, to sustain their spirits in this knowledge, and of not wanting to die without ever having made love. An anachronistic concept today, but one which many of the female contributors have been perfectly frank about. It was not the done thing, particularly if you wanted a white wedding, but whatever you decided, it was agony making the decision. And if your sweetheart died, you had to live with the guilt of perhaps not having loved them enough, or at least wishing you had been more courageous in flouting social convention. The letters in this book, and the many hundreds that could not be included, all convey something of the extraordinary intensity and heightened emotion of the war years, and give us a unique insight into the courage with which ordinary men and women lived their lives.

On the whole, we are no longer letter-writers. Telephones, faxes and e-mail have radically changed the part that letters used to play in people's lives. Without exception, the contributors to *Last Letters Home* have all spoken of the huge excitement of receiving the post, of the letters dropping onto the mat. Separation altered everyone's lives and relationships, and letters were a binding force: relationships were begun, sustained and ended by letter. Those who had never before written a letter to a loved one wrote their first, and often their last, letter during the Second World War. As one contributor put it, 'Letters are our last remaining links.'

Letters might have lessened the gap, but were no substitute for the person being there, not just for the big things, but to see the baby growing from day to day, to take part in the daily decisions we make together; to looking after one another during illness or grief. Letters could not be a substitute for physical presence. But they could and did speak of loss, love, loyalty, courage, loneliness, separation, hope and death, and they were a powerful focus in people's lives. They reflected, often quietly yet always bravely, what the writer felt about the war and needed to articulate.

Some writers clearly wrote to find out what they really felt, others to set the record straight, many to justify what they were doing and to make sure that their loved ones understood how they felt about them, in a way in which they could never, outside the war, have spoken or written. In some cases, when the person did not come home, these letters have become the recipient's most precious possession. They are, after all, all that remains of the writer, the last tangible evidence that the person ever existed, particularly for those whose bodies were never found.

The recall of the contributors has been astonishing, even though they are talking about the events of fifty years ago. The clarity and detail with which they remember the background to the letters, and the actual receiving of the letters – where they were, what they felt, who was with them, down to what they were wearing – only reinforces the crucial role the letters played and still play in their lives.

In this climate there were few certainties, but the writers wanted, *needed* to believe in a present and a future. They could write with certainty of their love, of how even separation could be turned to advantage. Many couples I spoke to believed – and still do – that the separation and letter-writing was the making of their relationship. It showed people what they meant to each other, and the separation, being something they had endured and survived, both individually and together, proved a rock-solid base for many relationships. Many of the couples have not spent a night apart since.

One contributor asks: 'How much love is generated by the fear of danger to another person?' An immeasurably large amount is clearly the answer, but, once generated, it had its own momentum and could not be extinguished by the arrival of peace. The shared experience of war is a hugely potent force.

Not unnaturally for the survivors still writing as the end of the war became imminent, a fresh set of realities – imponderables – began to dawn. The reality of the reunion, so long desired, no longer seemed to be the uncomplicated, single greatest wish on the horizon.

A different person would be coming home from the one who had gone away. They, in turn, would be coming home to a different person. Women were going to have to relinquish jobs and authority, men were coming back to who knew what? The uncertainties of peace, of finding a job, meeting your child as a stranger, picking up a life that probably no longer existed. This uncertainty, while not surprising in itself, I found in marked contrast to the certainties the

writers managed to express at the height of the war, and when in
most danger. More times than I can remember, I have read letters
and diaries resolute in their calmness, their faith, their hope,
expressing the most extraordinarily complex human emotions at a
time when death is the foregone conclusion waiting to happen, but
still the writer is intent upon telling his family what they mean to
him, what he has tried to do in life, to what purpose, and where he
has succeeded and failed. What has astonished me even more than
the substance of the letters, has been the maturity of the writers.
And yet many had barely reached manhood, most in their early
twenties. It is as though the natural lifespan has been accelerated
and all experience has been crammed into a fraction of the time it
would customarily take. Thus were the writers able to communicate
with the wisdom of youth and experience of age at once, with a
compelling force, certainty and maturity at the heart of everything.

The way in which these last, or final, thoughts were conveyed is
as individual as the writers. Some wrote 'last letters' to be given to
a loved one in the event of their death, either penning them days,
months, or even years before the event, and safekeeping them in the
meanwhile. Others wrote letters they never knew would be their
last. And some wrote what I still feel are the sentiments of a last
letter either at a particular stage of the war and their correspondence, or in dribs and drabs throughout their letters.

I have not included just those letters that spelt the end of a life,
a relationship, a correspondence. Often the most moving ones were
written when one writer or both knew of the man's imminent
return and their reunion; in one case a letter to a wife-to-be after a
return from prisoner-of-war camp completed the correspondence,
and anticipated their new life together without the need for letters.

In several cases, where women have had letters they wrote
returned after the addressee has gone missing or died, they have
burned their side of the correspondence. Keeping the loved one's
letters has proved difficult but possible to bear, but not their own.
Again, there have been huge differences in the contributors' ability
to reread the letters. While some have left them in trunks for
thirty, forty or fifty years, others have needed either the comfort of
keeping them to hand and rereading them, or the reminder, the

memory, the savouring of what their love felt like for each other at the time, and reliving the moment.

It has been a unique privilege to meet, interview, talk, and write letters to all the contributors to this book. It is they who have really written it, in telling their stories, making public their correspondence.

As a result, more of us will be aware during the fiftieth anniversary celebrations of the end of the Second World War of the extraordinary way in which people kept their parents, wives, sweethearts, husbands, children and families in touch, through the written word, during a period of our history when the pen became the most powerful tool in most people's possession.

PART I

Parents
&
Children

PAT WALLIS, SUE SWAN & TED BAKER

Frederick Lorraine Formidable Baker – Ted for short – and his wife Ruby had two children: Pat, and her brother Peter, who grew up to become the drummer Ginger Baker. Before Pat was born, her father had wanted a son, but he was soon besotted with his baby daughter.

Pat has fond memories of her father. She remembers him dressed in his uniform, taking down signals, and her last memory is of him going out of the front door with his kit-bag. He had been in the forces only ten months when he was killed. Pat was four.

For a year her mother and Ted's sister Sue had to live with the possibility of his death, yet without the certainty of it. Ruby included the official letter to her sister-in-law when she wrote to tell her what the War Office feared had happened. Sue was Ted's only sister; they were very close, and had written to each other since he'd joined up.

130 Southwood Road

Dear Sue,

Thanks for your letter I have been debating whether to tell you my latest news hence the delay. Please my dear try to be brave it's bad news. I'm quoting the War Office's reply to my enquiry for news.

REGARDING YOUR HUSBAND SIG. M. F. BAKER 2385113 I AM DIRECTED TO INFORM YOU, WITH DEEP REGRET, THAT IT IS FEARED FROM INFORMATION RECEIVED FROM THE MILITARY AUTHORITIES OVERSEAS THAT SGM. F. BAKER WAS KILLED IN ACTION, ON THE ISLAND OF LEROS. THESE REPORTS ARE BEING URGENTLY INVESTIGATED.

I AM TO CONVEY TO YOU AN EXPRESSION OF SINCERE SYMPATHY IN THE DISTRESS THIS LETTER MUST INEVITABLY CAUSE YOU AND TO ASSURE YOU THAT A FURTHER LETTER WILL BE SENT TO YOU IMMEDIATELY THE INVESTIGATIONS ARE COMPLETED.

I was coming, Sue, but I can't bear to talk about it yet awhile without crying and I wanted to help you to be brave but I know I can't. I know just how it's going to hurt you and I'd give a good deal to save you the pain but you must pay the price of loving him as I must. If only Geoff were home to ease your hurt but you have got to be brave and bear it alone. Try to get comfort as I have tried from his last words to me, 'If anything happens to me be brave and proud of me and remember I wasn't afraid of death and also that I hate tears.' Its hard cold comfort but so typical of the boy we knew. You had him longer than me and I had him longer than his two dear kids. I shan't tell them. I won't until they begin to realise, perhaps by then it won't hit them so hard. You'll be crying I know by now, have a good hard howl up Sue, it will make you feel a lot better in the end. God works in strange ways his wonders to perform and one day maybe we'll catch a glimpse of the reason for what now seems so cruel and unjust. I have written to your mum and dad and being the hard clear seeing person that you know, I feel this will not hurt them so badly as it's hurting you and I. That I suppose is a wicked thing to say but as always you will find the grain of truth there. I'm so terribly sorry for you as you loved in a way that few sisters can love and I know he thought the world of you too. If it can be of any help to you you know that you can always share his kids with me, if anything happened to me you are the one I should like to think of as taking my place, I can't say more than that. I'm tougher than you or shall I say the exterior is harder to pierce.

Anyway, I'm taking this thing as bravely as I can carrying on at work as I must always do now and trying to distract my thoughts with plans for the children's Xmas. You have an open invitation for Xmas or any part of it that you won't be sharing with your in-laws.

I know that Mrs. Swan will help you as much as she can but you will find as we all do at times like these that no-one can help us as much as ourselves. Come as soon as you can but we must show a brave front to the kids. They torture me unwittingly every day with questions and remarks about him and so far I have kept a poker face and hedged as best I can. God Bless them, they after all will feel it in time more than any of us but I'm looking to Geoff to help them and I know he will. Dear old Geoff to me he is like a rock in a stormy sea, strong and comforting, he will make it up to you, Sue, you will see.

Well, my dear, I've tried to comfort you, I hope I have succeeded, it's made me feel better to write to you. God Bless and help you, you've always been a wonderful sister to me.

All my love,
Ruby

Ted was missing for a year before an officer discovered all the marked graves, Ted's among them, on the island of Leros in the Dodecanese and notified his family. Ted was one of a hundred men ambushed on the island. Eighty-five were killed. The Germans came in quickly by sea and by parachute, outnumbering the British four to one. The family were told afterwards that they had fought so valiantly that the German soldiers had thought they were a Panzer division. Ted was twenty-eight.

A year later, when Ted's death had been confirmed, Ruby wrote once again to her sister-in-law confirming the unthinkable:

My Dear Sue,

Well, my sister, I'm sorry to have to once again upset you but after this there will be no more bad news. It has finally been established that our beloved Ted, was killed in action on Nov. 15th 1943 on the island of Leros and he's buried there. That is all they can tell me as yet perhaps when the island is in our hands we will know more about how he died and whereabouts his grave is. The only thing is it's final and we can no longer hang on to any hope. I've had the death report (last Friday actually) I've only just been able to bring myself to tell you. Don't grieve too much dear he wouldn't want it, he'd be the first to dry our eyes and tell us that life must go on. He'll never die for you and I, Sue, when he looks at us, laughs at us, from the eyes of Peter. Remember the words 'They'll never grow old as we that are left grow old—'.

We'll always be able to remember a laughing red headed dare devil, straight and sincere, reckless and lovable, fearless and affectionate. We must now think of the two he loved best in the world Pete and Pat and bring them up as he would have wanted.

I must close now, as they are waiting for supper, Rose and Arthur I mean. I'll be seeing you soon.

Cheer up, old girl, we'll get by. God Bless and help you through.

Love Ruby xxx

Sue remembers receiving it vividly: 'We were such mates. I'll never forget that letter. I cried on the bus all the way to my evening class, and my friends there were all so upset they cried with me.'

Ruby also told her daughter Pat that her father had been killed: 'I was in my mother's bedroom by the dressing table when she told me. I remember feeling very numb, unreal, it was like being told a story. I was only five.'

Ted had been killed in November 1943, but some months earlier, in 1942, he had written three letters, one to each of his children and Ruby, to be opened in the event of his death. It wasn't until Pat was fourteen that her mother felt she was old enough to be given her letter:

Sunday, 4th October 1942

My Darling little Pat,

I have been thinking things over while waiting for my boat, and as I might not return, I think it is only right that you should have a letter from me which you can keep, to remember me by. I am writing this assuming you are now grown up, as you will not receive this till then. I can picture you as a lovely girl, very happy with lots of boy friends. I am finding it very hard to write this as I may never see you at this stage. You have always been the pride and joy of my life. I have loved you more than my life and at all times. As mother has told you perhaps, I was always afraid of losing you. Now the tables have turned the other way and I might be the one to get lost. But do not let this upset you if this is the case, as the love for a father only lasts up to the time a girl finds the man she wants and gets married. Well, darling, when this time arises I hope you find the right one and he will not only be a good husband to you, but will also make up for the fatherly love you have missed. At all times, lovie, be a pal to mother and look after her, do what you can to make her happy, as she has been and will always be, I am sure, the best little mother you will find on this earth. Don't be selfish or catty, remember there are others in the world as well as you. Try not to talk about people as this gets you disliked. When the pulling to pieces starts, walk out or turn a deaf ear, it will pay in the long run. Above all I want you to be a sport, to take up swimming, dancing and all the games in life you can get so much fun out of. Mother, I am sure, will do her best for you and see you get all the instruction she can afford. Always try to be a sister to Peter and John [Pat's cousin], they may pull your leg about different things. But the best way after all is to ignore them and do what you can for them. You will win in the end and be the best of pals. Well, darling, there is no more I can say, but to look after yourself where men are concerned, be wise and quick witted and only believe half they say, of course till you get the right one. Remember me as your dad and pal who worshipped the ground you walked on. Please don't do anything that will upset mother, and I shouldn't like you to. I will close now, my little ray of sunshine.

    Always loving you.
    Your Loving,
    Father.
    xxxxxxxxxxxx

I remember my mum coming into my bedroom and giving it to me to read, and saying, "It's what your dad left you." I used to read it a lot when I was worried or upset about something. It makes me feel my father's looking over me and keeping an eye on me. I still remember him as someone always jolly and laughing. Dad had been a builder by trade, specializing in fancy brickwork. He'd go and have a drink with his mates on his way back from work – but not if he was going to come home and kiss me. A fortune-teller told him he'd die early.'

Sunday 4th. Oct. 1942.

my Darling little Pat,

I have been thinking
things over while waiting for my
boat, & as I might not return, I
think it is only right that you
should have a letter from me
which you can keep, to remember
me by. I am writing this assuming
you are now grown up, as you
will not receive this till then.
I can picture you as a lovely
girl, very happy with plenty of
boy friends. I am finding it very
hard to write this as I may never
see you in this stage. You have
always been the pride & joy of my
life. I have loved you more than
my life at all times. As mother
has told you perhaps I was
always afraid of losing you.

Pat always wanted to go out to Leros to try to find her father's grave. A few years ago she and her husband went to the island. They climbed the hill to the cemetery, and, on stepping into it, were faced with hundreds of war graves. The first grave Pat made for turned out to be her father's.

'His letter has definitely made me think more about how to live than I would have done if I hadn't had it. It has made me very responsible. I have memories of him from what my mother has told me, but the letter is as if he is still alive, and at the time it brought his death home to me.'

Although her mother was known as one of the 'merry widows of Eltham' – with all the men dead, she and her girlfriends went out dancing together – she still had to bring up the children on her own, work, and dig her vegetables. Eventually, Ruby remarried, but Pat says her mother always talked about her father and no one ever took his place. Her aunt Sue confesses to feeling very bitter at losing her beloved brother, but Pat is certain that her father's untimely death has made her stronger. That treasured last letter has exerted an extraordinarily powerful influence over her life.

'It has made me think about my life and how to live it. It makes you stop and think about how you treat other people, he instilled that into me. It's as if he's still alive, still there, because of my last letter. I can't remember anything else he ever said to me. That letter filled that void. I would never have known how he felt about me otherwise. It could only have happened in times like that, getting a letter like that. I know I'm far luckier than a lot of daughters whose fathers never said things like that.'

This January, after filming at Pat's home in Kent, we set off with her and Sue for Leros. Pat had always said she would return and it was a trip that Sue, now eighty-three, had waited fifty-one years to make. After a night in Athens we arrived back at the airport to catch the aeroplane for Leros. There had been storms all night and we were told that our flight would be cancelled – the storms were right along the route to the island and on Leros itself. Having got so far, Sue could not believe our bad luck. We sat it out for a couple of hours, knowing that by mid-afternoon it would be too late to fly – Leros has one tiny runway with no landing lights for night flying. Somewhere, somehow a prayer was answered and in the early afternoon we boarded the fourteen-seater and finally landed in near monsoon conditions.

We had only one night on the island, so we went straight to the cemetery to film what we could in the pouring rain. Ted's grave is beautifully maintained in the pretty little cemetery that looks straight out onto the bay and the far side of the island. Pat and Sue went immediately to the grave. As Sue touched it, she told us that she finally felt at peace. It was worth the fifty-one-year wait.

PAT & BRIAN ROWBERRY, & THEIR BROTHER IVOR

In the summer of 1946, the makers of Basildon Bond writing paper held a competition for the Best Letter Written by a Member of the Forces during the Second World War. The writer of the winning entry was Private Ivor Rowbery from the 2nd South Staffs Regiment, who had been born and brought up in Wolverhampton. The letter had been sent in an envelope marked 'To the Best Mother in the World'. It was published in the *Tatler and Bystander* on 18 September 1946. Two years earlier, Ivor had been reported missing, and, subsequently killed, at Arnhem.

Dear Mom,

Usually when I write a letter it is very much overdue, and I make every effort to get it away quickly. This letter, however, is different. It is a letter I hoped you would never receive, as it is just a verification of that terse black-edged card which you received some time ago and which has caused you so much grief. It is because of this grief that I wrote this letter, and by the time you have finished reading it I hope it has done some good, and that I have not written it in vain. It is very difficult to write now of future things in the past tense, so I am returning to the present.

Tomorrow we go into action. As yet we do not know exactly what our job will be, but no doubt it will be a dangerous one in which many lives will be lost – mine may be one of those lives.

Well, Mom, I am not afraid to die. I like this life, yes – for the past two years I have planned and dreamed and mapped out a perfect future for myself. I would have liked that future to materialize, but it is not what I will but what God wills, and if by sacrificing all this I leave the world slightly better than I found it I am perfectly willing to make that sacrifice. Don't get me wrong though, Mom, I am no flag-waving patriot, nor have I ever professed to be.

England's a great little country – the best there is – but I cannot honestly say 'that it is worth fighting for'. Nor can I fancy myself in the role of a gallant crusader fighting for the liberation of Europe. It would be a nice thought but I would only be kidding myself. No, Mom, my little world is centred around you and includes Dad, everyone at home, and my friends at W'ton – *That* is worth fighting for – and if by doing so it strengthens your security and improves your lot in any way, then it is worth dying for too.

Now this is where I come to the point of this letter. As I have already stated, I am not afraid to die and am perfectly willing to do so, if by my doing so, you benefit in any way whatsoever. If you do not then my sacrifice is all in vain. Have you benefited, Mom, or have you cried and worried yourself sick? I fear it is the latter. Don't you see, Mom, that it will do me no good, and that in addition you are undoing all the good work I have tried to do. Grief is hypocritical, useless and unfair, and does neither you nor me any good.

I want no flowers, no epitaph, no tears. All I want is for you to remember me and feel proud of me, then I shall rest in peace knowing that I have done a good job. Death is nothing final or lasting, if it were there would be no point in living; it is just a stage in everyone's life. To some it comes early, to others late, but it must come to everyone sometime, and surely there is a better way of dying than that of rotting of old age.

Besides I have probably crammed more enjoyment into my 21 years than some manage to do in 80. My only regret is that I have not done as much for you as I would have liked to do. I loved you, Mom, you were the Best Mother in the World, and what I failed to do in life I am trying to make up for in death, so please don't let me down, Mom, don't worry or fret, but smile, be proud, be satisfied. I never had much money, but what little I have is all yours. Please don't be silly and sentimental about it, and don't try to spend it on me. Spend it on yourself or the kiddies, it will do some good in that way. Remember that where I am I am quite O.K., and providing I know that you are not grieving over me I shall be perfectly happy.

Well, Mom, that is all, and I hope I have not written it all in vain. Good-bye, and thanks for everything.

Your unworthy son, IVOR

P.S. In case the fact that I am buried on foreign soil is worrying
you, here is a poem, that I learnt years ago and have never forgotten.
It is called the 'Soldier'.

> If I should die, think only this of me:
> That there's some corner of a foreign field
> That is for ever England. There shall be
> In that rich earth, a richer dust concealed;
> A dust whom England bore, shaped, made aware,
> Gave, once, her flowers to love, her ways to roam,
> A body of England's, breathing English air,
> Washed by the rivers, blest by suns of home.
>
> And think, this heart, all evil shed away,
> A pulse in the eternal mind, no less
> Gives somewhere back the thoughts by England given.
> Her sights and sounds; dreams happy as her day;
> And laughter, learnt of friends; and gentleness,
> In hearts at peace, under an English Heaven.

Goodbye Mom,
God Bless You All

Ivor was only twenty-one when he wrote the letter, a year before his
death on 22 September 1944. His sister Patricia, called Pat, has the
original. They were brought up in Curzon Street, Wolverhampton. Brian,
Ivor's brother, remembers they always fought with each other, and that
while Ivor was his mother's favourite son, he was his father's. When Ivor
left school at sixteen, he went to work locally at the Boulton and Paul
aircraft factory, which made Defiant aircraft. At school he had been
excellent at maths, and started off as an accountant. Brian remembers that
his talent for writing had also been recognized at school, and that Ivor
was: 'Very, very independent with a good sense of humour. If he believed
in something he stuck to it, he was adamant.'

At eighteen he was called up, and joined the South Staffs Airborne.

hope that I have not written
it all in vain.

Goodbye, and Thanks for
everything
Your unworthy son
Ivor.

P.S. In case the fact that I
am buried on foreign soil is
worrying you, here is a poem,
that I learnt years ago and
have never forgotten.
It is called the "Soldier".

"If I should die, think only this of me
That there's some corner of a foreign
field,
That is forever England — and there
shall be
In that rich earth, a richer dust
concealed,

He survived the invasion of Sicily, and came home for a fortnight's leave in October 1943. His only other leave was a fortnight before Arnhem.

Pat says, 'He didn't talk to us about it, but I think he thought he was going to die. I think he was quite fatalistic, he saw it as something he'd got to do, and if he got killed in the process, so be it. If you dread doing something you find the strength and get it over and done with. He had a couple of girlfriends, Margaret in Birmingham, and a Land Army girl from Lincoln where he'd been stationed. He felt he'd crammed a lot into his short life. He was really close to our mum, who always favoured the boys over the girls.'

In September 1944 Ivor was reported missing and in the following May he was presumed dead. He is buried in the cemetery at Oosterbeck near Arnhem.

Pat and Brian's mother refused to believe Ivor had died: '. . . because our father was a prisoner of war in World War I, and I suppose she couldn't help but believe the same had happened to Ivor, and she was going through it all again. She didn't believe it for years, even after we'd had confirmation. She never locked the back door at night, because she said Ivor might come home at any time of night. It must have been twenty years before she really accepted it. Our dad had finally come home, and she must've imagined the same had happened to Ivor.'

Pat remembers their mother saying that Ivor would not come back if he was maimed as he wouldn't want to be a burden to anyone. But it wasn't until her father died, that her mother finally seemed able to believe that Ivor, too, was dead and was able to grieve for both of them.

The day Mrs Rowbery received official notification of Ivor's death was ten years to the day since her son Gordon had drowned at the age of seven. She put an obituary in the local Wolverhampton paper, the *Express and Star*:

Ivor (South Staffs Airborne), eldest son of Mr. and Mrs. A. Rowbery, 68 Curzon Street, reported missing at Arnhem, now reported killed September. Will always be so proudly and lovingly remembered by mom, dad, sisters and brothers. To the world just another soldier; to me, all the world. Mom. Also treasured memories of our little Gordon, who left us without goodbye ten years ago today.

Brian didn't read Ivor's letter to their mother until it came out in the *Tatler*, and was sent to him as a soldier stationed in Trieste. 'I read it in the barracks, in late '46, I'll always remember it. I was very moved indeed, I cried; very moved and very proud. I knew there was no way I could have written a letter like that.'

Pat feels that Ivor was determined to make their mother proud of him. 'Times were hard, and he believed he hadn't done as much for her as he would have liked. She cried a lot when she got the letter, and gave it to me to read, but she *never* talked about it. She was very bitter, because she'd lost two sons, and in some peculiar way she blamed her daughters for being girls. I recorded the letter for Mum on tape when she went blind, and she listened to it a lot.'

SHELIA WHEBLE
& HER SON
TRISTRAM JOHN

Sheila Wheble, who died nearly two years ago, wrote a diary in the form
of a letter to her baby son Tristram John, which she kept until the end of
the war. She did not write it every day, but as and when she felt the need
to communicate a sense of what the war was doing to her, her family, and
the wider world. What she hoped was that if she were not to survive it,
her son Tristram John would be able, when he was older, to see exactly
what their life together had been like, and to find out about the mother
he would, by then, no longer remember: 'I wanted you to know me a
little should I be taken from you.'

A son has been born to Captain and Mrs. Tristram Wheble and
there is much rejoicing at the carrying of a name, and a family, that
would otherwise have died out . . .

    . . . What a world to be born into, my little Tristram John.
What a strange, unhappy, beautiful, tragic world . . . There is
hardly a corner now where peace is still maintained. The world is a
vast battlefield where men fight savagely in sandy desert, in knotted
jungle, in lonely islands, in shattered streets, in rugged mountains
and in the icy snows of a Russian winter. All the world over women
are being raped and violated, men are being tortured and slain,
children are bombed and machine-gunned, homes are wrecked and
families torn asunder. For love of peace we fight the bloodiest war
of all.

    . . . This book, little Tristram John, is written for you. If
anything happens to me at least it will tell you that I love you
very dearly, and remind you that love is eternal, and that one
day we shall be together again, if not in this world, certainly in
the next. Into this book I shall write my hopes, my prayers and
my innermost thoughts and wishes as they come, and always as I
write a great prayer and longing burns within me, that by the
time you are old enough to understand things we shall have peace
again, peace for you to be happy in, darling, you and all other
babies —

Sheila writes of carting T.J.'s little bed down the stairs and into the broom
cupboard when the doodlebugs were at their worst. Night after night,

from about 9 p.m. to 7 a.m., they would lie curled up in the cupboard, cramped, cold, aching all over, numb and miserable and haunted by the ever-present and terrible fear that 'we might never see the Glory of the Morning.'

A grey look appeared on people's faces that hadn't been there before; one learnt to sleep by day as much as possible for sleep by night was unknown!

She conveys the raids and their impact vividly; the fear, the noise, the relentlessness, but also the anger and determination that her fear engendered, determination to survive with her son at a time when death seemed inevitable.

Some time before the Flying Bombs started just before 'D Day' actually we had a very nasty time here indeed. It wasn't surprising we had expected it. The only surprising thing about it was the fact that the Huns hadn't attacked us sooner and oftener and on a much larger scale. Outside, the sea was a mass of ships. Landing barges of every shape and size and sort and wind craft so extraordinary that we couldn't even begin to guess what they were for. Never have I seen so many ships it was difficult to see an inch of water between them! What a target! Night after night, day after day, we waited for Hun to start his bombing attacks but they never came! At last, however, they began. Not the tremendous raids we had expected but scattered 'nuisance raids' by quite a few planes which, in spite of the smallness of their scale, caused not a few casualties and quite a lot of damage. It was then that they began to deliberately attack the Isle of Wight. We had never been deliberately attacked before. The bombs we had had, had mostly been meant for Portsmouth or had been dropped hurriedly on us whilst the planes made their escape while the going was good. Now we got the real thing and it was *not* pleasant!

I shall never, never forget that first dreadful night! The siren went and very shortly afterwards we heard the sound of planes and distant gunfire. I took you downstairs still sleeping and put you in your bed under the stairs. There was the far-off 'Crump, crump' of heavy bombs. Soon the guns from Yaverland and Culver took up the chorus and the sound of German planes could easily be heard coming closer. We waited for Nodes to join in. Pretty soon she did. 'Bang' that was Nodes! Then followed a terrible quarter of an hour. The noise outside was appalling. A.A. guns, cannonfire, tracer bullets, machine-gunning and all the time the sound of planes diving down on top of us or weaving in and out of the searchlights trying to escape their beams. Added to this the bombs were falling steadily. The whole house shook to its foundations. The walls of our cupboard quivered and shuddered. This went on, at ten minute intervals all night long. The planes, as usual came over in relays at intervals. Wave after wave of heavy German bombers overhead. I know of no feeling quite so terrifying as that feeling of complete and utter helplessness that comes during a raid when one is lying in shelter or cupboard completely at the mercy of the Hun without a chance of hitting back. The sound of the broken throb of those planes steadily approaching is one that will haunt me to my dying day. I shall never forget the horror of it.

These raids went on for a fortnight. We slept, cramped and chilled in our cupboard. Waiting whilst the minutes ticked by for those first grey fingers of dawn-light to tell us that our ordeal was nearly over and rising thankfully to our feet at the sound of the 'All Clear' heavy-eyed, aching in every limb, worn-out and weary – but . . . alive! One night was almost unendurable. The noise outside was such a jumble of sounds that it was impossible to make out what was really happening. Bombs were whistling down, sometimes they sounded like falling planes and seemed to be coming down right on top of us. The Hun seemed to be driving on Nodes using their cannons and machine-guns as well as dropping their bombs, all our guns were firing and the sky was lit up with the beams of countless searchlights and the brilliant crimson splashes of tracers.

Suddenly, there was an appalling whistling sound, I can't possibly describe it properly, it sounded exactly as if a plane were twisting and turning and falling faster and faster down towards the ground. Towards us! I was, for the first time in my life, really frightened but couldn't show it because of you. My knees felt like water, I had never wanted to live so desperately as then when I believed death to be inevitable. You looked up from your little bed, an adorable, flushed-with-sleep little face and starry eyes and cried 'That's a Big One, Mummy!' I managed to say 'Yes, Darling.' How endless those seconds seemed. Endless. At last . . . crump, crump. The house shivered and shook to its foundations, the cupboard walls seemed to be caving in but it was over! They'd missed us.

A few moments later the telephone rang. I remember stumbling with stiff and aching knees, to the telephone. With fingers that couldn't still their trembling I picked up the receiver and heard an agitated voice saying 'I can't get any answer, I can't get any answer.' I managed to give a squeaky 'Hullo' and heard a fervent 'Thank God, here they are' from the other end! 'Are you alright?' said the voice. 'Rather', I replied, 'Where did they fall?' 'Right over your house', he answered, 'one on the golf-links, just missed Woodnutts, the other in the mill-pond, we watched them coming down, they've fallen up by the Priory too and in the fields round Nodes; been falling all over the place, mostly in the fields or sea though as far as we can tell.' So that was that. Thank God they'd missed us, what a night! Next day I took you away to Guildford for a month, it was quiet there. I brought you back a week after D-Day. All was quiet in the Island again but two days after we left Guildford, out of the blue came the Flying-bombs. All round Guildford they fell. Epsom, Ewell, Ripley; our friends at Caxtons Hotel where we'd been staying spent every night under the stairs for weeks, the noise was appalling, their nerves frayed for lack of sleep. In the Island they didn't start for a month and then only came at night, at least we had quiet days, while on the mainland night and day the people lived a nightmare of terror and uncertainty. A War Nursery near Guildford got a direct hit. I read the accounts Dead Babies, oh so many of them, and, what struck one as even more pathetic somehow, amongst the piles of debris, toys and tiny shoes lying, the beloved Teddy Bears, and the tiny owners, my God, how savage it made us. The Hun will never understand that he cannot cow us into submission or terrorise us into surrender, the fiercer and more vicious his attacks, the stronger we become, the more resolute, the more determined. So it was now – the Flying bombs and, later, the rockets, did nothing to frighten us they made us more furious and more determined to defeat the Hun utterly.

The last entry was written on 31 October 1945, safe in the knowledge that Tristram John would not have to read the diary as though it were his mother's last letter. The war was over, and he and his mother had survived.

My Dear Tristram John,

I haven't written enough I know about the War years. Future generations, if this book survives, will want to know how we felt and how we lived in England during those dreadful years. Well, the purpose of this book was not to dwell on War but, purely and simply, to tell you about your Mother!

I wanted you to know me a little should I be taken from you. I wanted you to know a little of my childhood and to learn my likes and dislikes and meet, through these pages, some of my friends. Had I died you might never have known anything about me. You might have met people who would tell you that I was pretty or attractive or gay or quiet, but none of them would have really known me. In this book I have tried, and shall continue to try, to point out to you all that I have loved in this World, and believe me I love it all, the people and the things! Also, this has been a way of escape for me. I have been able, when writing in this book, to forget, for a while, the stress and struggle of the War and find peace again in the quiet England of my childhood amongst the friends of my youth.

Before she died, Sheila lodged her diary with the Imperial War Museum and when I got in touch with Tristram John, to discuss the inclusion of some of it in the book, he knew nothing about it. He had vague memories of 'drinking gallons of cocoa under the stairs in the broom cupboard when the doodlebugs came', and of his mother saying she had sent a diary to the museum. Though it is very precious to him, he has never read it. I hope he will now.

ERIC RAWLINGS

A short piece in St. Andrew's Church magazine in April 1942, tells of the death of Eric Rawlings. The church, in Alexandra Park in North London, was where Eric had been a choirboy: he died at the age of twenty-one, killed in action with the RAF, and was buried in Lincolnshire. His father, Norman, said of him, 'He perfectly fulfilled all we ever hoped of him.'

Knowing that he would be engaged in operations over Germany, and therefore in constant danger, Eric wrote a letter to his parents, Marjorie and Norman, which he entrusted to his brother Norman to give to them in the event of his death:

Dearest Folks,

Now that I'm on operational work and admitting that the risk is fairly considerable, I thought I would just put a few words on paper which you could keep as a remembrance in case anything should happen to me.

In the revoltingly chaotic world today where everyone is fighting and killing everyone else, it has always been wonderful just to take my thoughts from worldly beastliness and to think of the things which I revere and esteem most in the world – my family and my home.

Love is such a very difficult thing to express here and now on paper, but I only hope that I've made you all understand and realise the depth of my love and the gratitude for everything which you have done for me.

Whenever there's fighting going on anywhere, you can always hear the words from people not involved – 'Half of them don't know what they're fighting about anyway.' Which is usually true. Well, I know what I'm fighting for. I'm fighting so that in the future people will have the chance to live as happily as we all did together before the War without interference. Where young un's like myself could make the most of the marvellous opportunities which you gave me for twenty years and for which I know you made many sacrifices. God bless you all, and may everything turn out right in the end.

God bless you again,

Your adoring son and 'Little One'.

After finding this letter, I traced Eric's niece Barbara Cookson. Although she never met her uncle – she wasn't born until after his death – she had been intrigued to find out exactly what had happened to him. 'I found Eric's last letter when I was sorting through my grandfather's papers – he survived all his children – and I remember thinking, this was twenty years ago now, I must do some work on this when my children are at school. I'm a very nosey person. That's why a couple of years ago, I finally decided to follow it up. I'm hooked on family trees, fascinated not so much by dates, but by what families actually did, and I've traced back to 1300, 1600 and 1700 with branches of my family and my husband's. I made enquiries at the Ministry of Defence, and they wrote and told me the following. Eric was the wireless operator and air gunner on Wellington R1463 of 150 Squadron based at Snaith in Yorkshire. On the night of 21/ 22 February 1942, the aircraft was returning from a raid, when it flew into a 400-foot hill at Asterby Top Farm in Asterby, Lincolnshire. The cause of the crash was thought to have been altimeter lag as it was reading 900 feet at the time of the accident. Three other members of the crew are reported to have been killed, and one injured.'

PART II

Brothers
&
Sisters

ANTONY
&
IVOR BRETT-JAMES

Antony Brett-James was born in 1920 and his brother Ivor in 1922. They were both educated at Mill Hill, where their father Norman taught history. Antony went on to read languages at Cambridge, but his university career was interrupted by the war. On 17 May 1940, his mother Gladys wrote to him sympathizing with him that he had to break off his Cambridge life, and delay his career:

But however disappointed one may feel I am quite sure you feel that it is your straight duty to join up and take your share in freeing your country from this wild beast that is crushing all joy and life out of all countries. What chance is there for anyone until we stay this power of evil? If only a force as strong as this could be turned into one for good! We are so thankful that these last 2 years have given you such a broadened outlook on life. They have taught you much and given you a power to face up to the future with confidence and good cheer.

Antony began what was to be five and a half years in the Royal Corps of Signals, serving in Egypt, Syria, Iraq, India and Burma. Ivor joined the 9th Durham Light Infantry on leaving school and was sent to Africa to await orders. Then, to his parents' horror, he was sent to Sicily, leaving in such a hurry that he had with him only one pack and the clothes he stood up in.

Earlier that year, on 17 May, Ivor had written to Antony about their letters:

Last night I read for over two hours your letters to Mum and Dad from about November right up to date. You say that you do not find it easy to write letters, but one would never guess it by reading them. The real trouble is that yours are so much better than mine that they invite invidious comparison. You certainly are almost the only person I get any pleasure in writing to . . . Also this might be my last leave.

On 1 June he wrote to his brother from home, while on fourteen days' embarkation leave. Their mother wrote to Antony the next day:

You can guess what a busy time we are having. It's so lovely having Ivor and I try not to think of the future. I couldn't expect to keep him in this country.

Three weeks later, seemingly determined to use their correspondence for their mutual morale, Antony's mother writes:

I hope this letter is long enough, darling! We think so much of you. I feel we keep very near to each other through our mail; more we can't hope for at present. We must face a week at a time, and remain undaunted, however bad the news is. Keep optimistic. We shall win, however long it takes.

The letters which follow, written between 4 August and 5 October 1943, are Antony's and Ivor's letters home, together with their parents' replies. Antony's mother writes to him on a short break in Clevedon, where despite the old friends, the welcome of the hotel, and the walks on the beach, her main preoccupation is with the 'great shock' of Ivor having been sent to Sicily. As so often, mundane everyday business must take its place alongside the shocking reality of war.

Ivor's valedictory message to Antony is single and uncompromising, nothing else matters, no glory, no honour, but 'try to come out of this bloody war alive and unmaimed' – 'all that matters is to get back with a whole skin.'

Ivor Brett-James to Norman & Gladys Brett-James

4th August 1943

I have recently been a bit troubled with septic 'desert sores' and my arms and knees are all bandaged up. It looks all very impressive but it is not at all serious, only very inconvenient. They seem to be very common here and are caused by bad water, dirt and bugs. Naturally we all say that we have been wounded.

Our lives at times are completely topsy turvy as we sleep by day, at least we would sleep if it were not for the flies and ants, and by night we feed, wash and try to stay awake.

I have now got another tin box, which started life holding ammunition and in which I can put some of my kit. All kit one can get hold of out here from the Q.M. is free, as at times you can't help losing it.

Today I have been distributing the first NAAFI stores we have seen here and managed to get a bottle of lime juice for myself as the others had beer and whisky. Out here we wear our peaked caps all the time. My topee was left in Africa unworn, and when a news cameraman came up to the front line to 'shoot' us he told us to put our steel helmets on as it looked more realistic. So one day you might see me on the flicks! Today also I undressed, washed and took off my boots for the first time in almost a week. It makes you feel ten years younger.

Gladys Brett-James to Antony Brett-James

Clevedon, 7th August 1943

We had a very warm welcome here from many old friends. The chief attraction of this hotel is the friendliness of the residents. No hotels are really comfortable; there are so many economies, but we are getting on well, and I get extra rations of butter and cheese for Dad. I brought apples and tomatoes. None of these things can be bought unless you are registered. Of course it's a great advantage having Auntie and the cottage . . .

You will have heard about Ivor. It was a great shock to hear he was in Sicily. I expect it surprised him too. I feel very anxious, and his regiment has been mentioned as doing specially well. Apparently he is with the 9th D.L.I. Whether this is for the duration is not clear. This mixing up of regiments seems customary and tiresome, and I know will annoy Ivor. His address is vague, and he told us to use the B.N.A.F. one. It's no use giving it to you, it changes too often. His luggage is all in Africa and he has only a pack. Something is jettisoned with every move. He doesn't expect to see any of it again. It's almost comic when we reflect on the care with which we bought and packed, and creased the trousers etc. Now he has only what he stands up in. I hoped he wouldn't be in the fighting for a bit, but there he is, and we must pray for his safety.

Ivor Brett-James to Antony Brett-James

8th August 1943

Still no mail from anybody, but I have just been re-reading your last letters I got in England. In them you complain that you have seen no action as yet. When I left England you had already been abroad 18 months, but already out here in Sicily I have seen more than enough. You have missed nothing worthwhile and even if your present life is dull (it may be very different now) stick to it and try to come out of this bloody war alive and unmaimed. That is all that really matters. Not medals, Africa stars and all that cock. It is your brains that we want after the war, not your decorations.

You also lament the lack of anything better than a hurricane lamp to light your mess with. Well, we have no mess and no lamps, nor are we likely to have either for a long time. We have been eating by night and living in holes dug in the ground full of ants, fleas, lice, flies, mosquitoes, wasps, and a lot more, and as a result my body is one mass of festering sores and bites and I am swathed in bandages. My face is daubed with some purple muck and I cannot shave. For weeks at a time we have not even taken our boots off, let alone undressed, and two hours is a good night's sleep. We have been sweating in a climate as hot as Africa and when dead a man and a cow smell alike. The foulest smell on earth.

Reading that through it seems very petulant, almost abusive;

but it is true. You in the Sigs or anything else whom we watch in your trucks as we march along have little conception of what war is really all about.

All that matters is to get back with a whole skin.

Salud y Victoria

Ivor Brett-James to Norman and Gladys Brett-James

8th August, 1943

My last note to you was so very short that this one must try and make up for it . . .

Before the war this island must have been a delightful place to visit, with its beautiful scenery, friendly people and luxuriant vegetation. In the centre of the island the land becomes more bleak and considerably colder, but here there is really no difference most days between here and North Africa. Now of course there is no rain and the general colouring is brown with patches of green wherever there is an orchard, whether it be oranges, lemons, grapes or almonds. At the moment I am sitting in the shade of a 'mandel-baum', such a pretty little tree, and we have been humming Schumann's song about it. We have had some lovely bathing on the island, but like the whole Mediterranean it suffers in having no tide to wash the beach.

I have been wishing recently that I knew more of the ancient civilization of this island, for we have seen many ruins and build-ings and other signs of the home of the Doric school, but we have had little enough chance to inspect them in detail. The other day I was strolling over a deserted piece of country and chanced on a Penguin copy of 'Pygmalion' which I hastily added to my meagre library; it will be a great day when the first books from you get here!

One of my fellow officers is also a music fan and a dilettante singer of Lieder, so every night we wade through 'Schone Mullerin' or 'Winterreise' or some other Schubert songs. We then wander on to Schumann, Hugo Wolf and others. It makes a great relaxation, as it is the first music I have heard since I sailed. Although that day is not two months hence it seems like half a lifetime.

Occasionally we hear the BBC news and it gives one a funny feeling when you have the announcer saying what we have been actually doing. Frequently they get it all wrong, much to our fury.

Gladys Brett-James to Antony Brett-James

Clevedon, 11 August 1943

I am sitting in auntie's garden, sun and breezes, and I look over to the Kewstoke hills. Low tide with a white bank of foam on the wet sands; such a beautiful and peaceful view. As our Yorkshire friend says: 'I fair luv this place.' Dad has played bowls twice, so good for him. 2½ hours for a shilling. We are so happy at our hotel; for war it's very comfortable, plenty to eat, no choice, but I buy tomatoes and lettuce for Dad instead of puddings.

14 August 1943

Once again we have a wind free day and Dad and I are on the pier, sitting in the breeze and sun. The tide is very low, and I am reminded of many adventures on the beach, breakwater and rocks below. How we enjoyed it! Do you remember the day you got in the mud by mistake and ran to the bathroom and changed before I saw you! Children are still sailing boats and climbing rocks. Every generation does the same. The pier is very shabby.

Gladys Brett-James to Antony Brett-James

18 August 1943

We arrived home at 2 p.m. Our time at Clevedon has been as pleasant as ever, and we were sad to leave. The view from the hotel gives one such a sense of peace. Naturally Ivor was uppermost in our thoughts. He must have had a dreadfully gruelling experience, and now the Sicily show is done, we long to know he is safe. He was on August 8. We found an L.C. to greet us, but it was Aug. 4. I pray all is well. There's no glamour in war, he thinks. They will probably have a rest for a bit.

Gladys Brett-James to Antony Brett-James

29 August 1943

My darling Roly, How I wish I could spare you our sad news, but we share everything together. Ivor was killed in action on Monday Aug. 9th. He wrote to you last of all. His last to us was on the 4th. I hope it was all instantaneous. The news came this morning from the War Office, and altho' we had been very anxious this last week, it came as a stunning blow. Ever since the broadcast by Lewis Hastings a week or more ago, when he told us of the heavy casualties in the D.L.I. C Coy and the tremendous stand they had made and gave them such praise, our fears have been growing, but we have gone on hoping for good news. He was so thoughtful and wrote whenever he had the chance, and cabled once. It seems like a dream somehow. We can't do anything but face as bravely as we can this sorrow. Perhaps Ivor is saved further horror of war, for after Sicily who knows? We must not grieve for him, only that his happy and promising life is cut short. I feel so stunned and dare not think of details. I just give thanks for the beautiful 21 years we have had him. Ivor's love for you has been very great and it's been such a happiness to us that you were both such friends. I know how sad and lonely you will feel. It's a very great shock, and I feel more for you than I can tell you. Ivor would not have us grieve, so let us only give thanks for happy memories, and then carry on. I am so distressed that Ivor never had any letters after he left England. They might have helped him. If we have any particulars we will tell you. We decided not to cable; it serves no purpose, and letters are about as quick . . .

You make no mention of people. I want you to make a great effort to make friends. Don't bottle this sorrow up inside you; talk

to someone. It does help so. I pray that you will come safely
through this war, do your duty, and may God bless and keep you
from harm. Our friends here are most kind. I am sure we shall
adjust ourselves, so do not worry about us, darling. This is a big
sorrow we all share together. Devoted love from your Mum.

Norman Brett-James to Antony Brett-James

29 August 1943

My dearest Antony, Mum and I are both writing to you by the
same Sunday post, to tell you that our dearest Ivor has 'gone; killed
in action on 9 August, the day after he wrote that letter from Sicily
which we forwarded to you. This morning at 10.30 the Post Office
rang me up with a telegram from the War Office. Sympathy from
the Army Council, signed by the Under Sec. of State. It doesn't
seem possible that we have lost that radiant beautiful son. It hardly
bears thinking about, but we all have to be very brave. We are so
sorry that you should have to face this news alone. Directly I heard,
after telling Mum, I rang up Carters and Aunts. Stanley arranged
to do my duty from 12–2, so as to leave me with Mum for lunch.
Ada came in from 12–1 and was most affectionate and kind. At 2
I went to C2 and was on with Brian Miller. We had invited him
and his wife to tea, so we went on with it. It broke up our thoughts
a bit and helped us over a difficult hour or so. It is impossible to
look round without being reminded of our dear boy. He has had a
short innings at the front, but he has given us 21 glorious years. I
don't think either he or you have ever given us a moment's anxiety.
We have been blest in our two boys.

And I feel, as Tennyson wrote: ''Tis better to have loved and
lost than never to have loved at all.' Try and look on the bright side
of things, if you can, and bear in mind that Ivor has made the
supreme sacrifice for a splendid cause.

It is no good telling you not to worry, for I know what
tremendous pals you were, and how you looked forward to the post-
war world. But God will, I know, give us strength to bear this

blow, and to carry on in spite of it. Don't think of the situation and all that it involves in too much detail. I feel sure he was killed instantaneously. We both here felt, even down at Clevedon, that something had happened; and have been growing more apprehensive ever since. And now it has happened. It makes us all the more dependent on your love, so take very good care of yourself. Mum is being marvellous, and I know we shall pull through. We mustn't let this sorrow get us down.

Your very loving Dad

Gladys Brett-James to Antony Brett-James

1 September 1943

I imagine that the letters have reached you in sequence and that the sad news of Ivor's death has reached you. We do of course feel very forlorn, and it will take a long time before one can adjust oneself. At present the sense of loss and futility is uppermost. I am so proud of you both, and Ivor with so short a time of preparation has made the greatest of all sacrifices. That this is not in vain we feel sure and the day will come when Peace comes into the hearts of men. I know how much he hated war and all the misery it brings. He loved all beautiful things, but when his time came he forgot himself and was glad to go overseas. I don't think one can know what war is unless one is in the midst of it, but I do know that Ivor's courage never failed him. Perhaps it is best for him to go now; worse might come which would bruise his soul. I try, and I know you will too, to feel that all is best for Ivor. You said a while back that you felt that Ivor had developed very much. He had altered quite a lot, lost all his hasty sulky mood, and become more thoughtful, companionable, and quick in thought and action – above all, reliable. His judgment was sound, and I know, had he lived, he would have gone far.

You always thought this. Well, his admiration of you was as warmhearted and sincere. We talked much of you. I am glad he loved you so. It's always the greatest joy to parents when they have the affection and confidence of their children, and Dad and I realize how fortunate we are. I am determined to rise above this sorrow. Ivor has done his bit and we must do ours. He would hate to feel we were unhappy. It will be hard. I feel him very very near, and his photos smile at us from every corner.

We are so surrounded by love and kindliness up here. All our friends have been in, and oh! so many have written.

Antony Brett-James to Norman and Gladys Brett-James

17 September 1943

It was seven o'clock, when the sun was very low, and my mind and body wearied of the petty irritations of the day's work, and I stood outside my Signal Office, ready to go to my shanty to bath and change. On the table 3 familiar welcome letter-cards, pale blue and the well known hand. Mum's I picked up first and read the date, 30 Aug. I slit the cover and rumpled it open. 'My darling Roly, How I wish I could spare you our sad news.' I read on, uncomprehending much. 'But we share everything together. Ivor was killed in action on Monday Aug 9th. He wrote to you last of all.' I read it ordinarily as if you had written nothing unusual – it was not till I had started Dad's that the fact really hit me, staggered me, so that I went to my office adjoining, unable to see the page through the tears. I had to get away – my orderly I dismissed, and my bath. I hastened into slacks, hid my sorrow from my room mate in the dimness of the hurricane lamps, stuffed three yellow tangerines into my pocket, and walked into the near darkness. Dinner I could not face, so I wandered out over the grass, peeling and sucking the fruit, thinking vaguely, uncontrollably but not unwittingly, at moments incoherently, blinded, agonised, and then lucid to scorching point. I wandered to and fro, alone, too much alone, with no one to turn to but God. No one being I really care to share it with, so I have returned to my bedside and write thus above a pair of lamps. The tears have gone, though to read your letters or to reflect brings them welling up again. I am at peace with exhaustion, battling to know what to write to you both – I can only say exactly what has pulsed in my brain these last two hours.

I must have been riding in Darjeeling when it happened, I in cloud, and rain, he in great heat and sun. Although I was vaguely worried by the fact that he was in action, I had not feared as greatly as before he had left England – then I cared far more for his safety than for mine, and rather dreaded his going overseas. Above all, I realize that, whatever I feel now, and that is stunning and wounding enough, the full weight of the blow will not come upon me until the day I come home, if God spares me, and find no Ivor waiting for me to share the post-war world . . .

Keep, as I know you will, every belonging and paper of his – among my drawers you will find many letters from him, and in mine to him are many ideas I never expressed to you. I feel too that, if ever I have a son, his name shall be Ivor in memory. Always the future hits me in the eye – no sister-in-law and nephews; countless plans we hoped to realize.

His last letter card to me was written on the eve of his death – he said that the only thing that counts is to survive. 'We want your brains, not your medals.' Well, he had brains in plenty, and exceptional powers of passing on to others his knowledge. I have remarked on that quality before. He had lost the stiffness in society and had charm – his look was acute and penetrating, his head striking. He was a great lover of beauty, of worthwhile possessions, and that love reflected beauty in himself. He bore the stamp of nobility, of the *elite*, I feel . . .

I am grateful for so many memories. My regret that I had seen him so little in the last 3 years – just brief leaves, a few days at Cambridge, my embarkation leave and no more. I still don't know how to believe it. We shared so many interests. I am trying to think which piece of music best typifies him. I am thankful you sent no telegram. I was better off with 3 letters to grip at. I do hope you get more news of the last days. Ask for return of his kit. I have always been very proud of him, of telling others of him, and I must give thanks for his companionship in the past, though so much of the future is altered. The memory can never be taken from us, though the world is the poorer for his loss, and the new world needs men of his calibre. Sad that he had no letters the last weeks. His 21st was a bit lonely, for his last one, but I am glad you had him almost to the last, with a brief spell abroad. I am sure he was a first-rate officer, and loved of his men. So fair always . . .

I won't write more now – be very courageous, and know how wonderfully I love you both, and shall always love Ivor as my only brother, though he be gone.

Gladys Brett-James to Antony Brett-James

5 October 1943

Your most wonderful airmail, written the night you heard about Ivor, came yesterday afternoon, and it is a relief to make contact and to know you have heard. I know just how desperately unhappy you will have felt, and it will take a very long time to heal over such a deep wound.

They tell me time is a great softener and healer, and I believe this will be so. It's so easy to give over to one's griefs and emotions, like biting a sore tooth, but we must keep our thoughts off all distressing details and remember Ivor as he was. You would have been prouder still if you had seen him the last 6 months, so keen and alert and thoughtful. He gave one the feeling of strength and inward calm.

You are quite right when you say we shan't feel the full weight of the blow until the time of reunion, but I am sure that when the time comes we shall be as courageous as we are trying to be now. It's a great thing to have a job that has to be done, and I am so thankful that leaves you little time for indulging in sadness and that uses your many talents and power of leadership . . .

I am so sorry he never heard of your promotion: he would have felt so proud. He always asked where you were. He will know now and be glad. We must always think of him as very near. I can't bear the idea of silence. He will go on living in our hearts always. 'Do not think they have been lost for ever. God did not lose them when

He gave them to us, and we have not lost them by their return. They hold His Right hand and walk in light; we hold his Left hand and walk in twilight, yet both are one.' I find that very comforting. It was in a booklet sent us by a Rev. Macbeath.

Lt. Col. Humphrey Wood wrote to the Brett-Jameses telling them in detail how Ivor had died:

I am writing to send you all my sympathy and that of the Battalion for the tragic loss you have sustained in the death of your son. He was killed leading his platoon – the forward platoon of the leading company in the Battalion just outside the village of Riposto. On rounding a bend in the road they were surprised by an enemy machine gun at fifty yards range. With no cover available nearby he was caught in the enemy fire, and I am glad to say can have known nothing of it. His C.S.M. was killed alongside him, and his Company Commander badly wounded just behind. It was a very cleverly concealed ambush and no fault of the platoon or their leaders. . . . He was buried where he fell . . .

Ivor had spent his twenty-first birthday in the line; he never received his twenty-first birthday mail, it was all returned to his mother. His parents had the following In Memoriam made:

In Memoriam
LIEUT. JOHN IVOR BRETT-JAMES
The Oxford and Buckinghamshire Light Infantry,
(Attached Durham Light Infantry)
Born at Ridgeway, Mill Hill, 20th July, 1922
Killed in Action in Sicily, 9th August, 1943.

We have been very touched by the extremely kind letters which we have received from all our friends at this time of tragic sorrow. It has come as a tremendous shock to us to hear of Ivor's death in action in Sicily, and his passing has left a blank in our lives that can never be filled. But we are very greatly supported by the thoughts and prayers of our friends, and we believe that we shall be given strength to bear up under our irretrievable loss. Ivor spent his 21st birthday in the line, and the four weeks he had in Sicily were mainly grim fighting. Soldiering was not natural to him: but he proved in the Essex Regt., at R.M.C., in the Oxford and Bucks. Light Infantry, and while attached to the Durham Light Infantry, that he possessed great natural powers of leadership.

He was a lover of Maps, and of the Countryside and Camp fires and of everything beautiful. His great hobbies were Scouting and Music; and a visit to the National Gallery Concerts, or to the Sadlers Wells Ballet, or a Gramophone Concert from Sibelius or Mozart, or a B.B.C. programme from the Albert Hall gave him his happiest hours. He was a very keen King's Scout, and loved Camp and the Dutch Jamboree, and he was very proud at being, like his brother, one of the King's Bodyguards at the Cenotaph on Armistice Day. His passing will mean as much to Antony as to any of us, as the two were tremendous chums, and had made plans to work together in the post-war world. A friend, in writing to us, referred to Ivor as bright, resourceful, upright, sympathetic and mature, and he was all that and more.

He took the war very seriously and made himself as proficient as it was possible to be. His death is part of the price we have to pay for a better world, and it is doubly hard that it is mainly from the young that war demands

> The love that never falters
> The love that pays the price
> That lays upon the altar
> The final sacrifice.

But we are proud that he faced death unflinchingly, we are grateful for the 21 glorious years of his life, and we thank God for every remembrance of our dearly loved son.

Yours very gratefully,

Gladys Brett-James wrote to her surviving son on 10 October 1943:

Wars are a tremendous shock to the young, such a tragic disillusion-
ment and a shattering of all their hopes and plans. And when Death
takes away their contemporaries it seems as if life was no longer
real. It all seems so unbelievable, and you only realize what applies
to you all. I can't believe that it's God's will that any of our boys
and girls should give their lives. They can serve their country so
much better by leading good, brave lives, but when such a world
chaos arises, brought about by man's greed and cruelty, there is no
alternative –

After his brother's death, Antony fought at Imphal and was mentioned in Dispatches. When he returned from the war he completed his
degree at Cambridge and began to write. He became an acknowledged
expert on Wellington and Napoleon. Later he became Head of the War
Studies Department and International Affairs at RMA Sandhurst. Some
years after my father, C. Day-Lewis, died, Antony and my mother began
to live together and did so until his death in 1984. My mother tells me
that she first saw the letters seventeen years ago and was 'profoundly
moved' by them. When Antony died she gave the letters to the Imperial
War Museum. Antony's other papers were already lodged there.

FLORA SCOTT
& HER BROTHER
MIKE

Flora Scott was born in Chester in 1912, one of a family of four brothers and four sisters. She was closest to her younger brother Mick, who was born four years later in 1916. When Mick was a schoolboy at Shrewsbury, he and Flora corresponded all the time. Flora was dyslexic and her schooldays were consequently extremely difficult, but she would write and tell him all the jokes going on at school, and send him the bits of poems she liked, as she had just discovered poetry. Mick longed to be a writer and everything he wrote he would send to Flora. In the holidays they had fun riding his bike, Mick on the bar and Flora pedalling; going bird's-nesting, paddling in a flooded field. Whatever they did, they did together.

After they left school Mick became a prep-school master and Flora took a job as a school matron; they dreamed of running their own school one day. When the war came, Mick joined the RAF and Flora still remembers how much Mick adored flying: 'It takes two years to train a pilot. Mick was flying on ops in nine months, in Bomber Command. They were sacrificing those ones at that stage to keep going. He wrote and said that I mustn't mind what happened to him, because he'd achieved his dream of learning to fly.' In 1940 he wrote to Flora:

The thought of coming to a sticky end does not worry me in the least and it ought not to worry you. Life is merely a passing phase in our development the rest of which is obscure at present, but undoubtedly there, if not in the accepted Christian sense.

Things like music are outside this life and we ought to be able to enjoy them more fully when we leave it.

It seems to me that in the air one will lose contact with all earthly things, and become part of the Universe and touch things spiritual, which are far finer.

Mick kept a diary throughout his training period, listing all the music he listened to and was moved by during his time off. The entry for 24 May 1941 is in red, marking his first operational flight. It was to be his last. He went missing over the North Sea and was never heard of again. The week before he had been to stay with Flora at her school in mid-Wales. The boys had all loved him.

'My mother rang up the headmaster, who sent his wife to tell me. "I've got something to tell you," she said, before hurriedly denying it by saying, "No I haven't, I take that back", and disappearing to the loo. She then plucked up the courage to tell me. As soon as he was killed I had a tremendous feeling he was with me. I feel sure that if you are close to someone they are with you till you can bear to let them go once they've died. I remember going out and playing golf and saying to myself "Look at this shot Mick," and feeling he was there. I went straight home, and Mother told me I mustn't upset my father by showing how shattered I felt. I remember him in turn saying to me, "I can't comfort your mother." Later he wrote to me saying, "I hate to see my favourite child in such distress."'

The year before, on 21 August 1940, anticipating death, Mick had written a last letter to their father, paying tribute to both his parents, and revealing the philosophy that had enabled him to fight in a war of which he had no desire to be a part.

21/8/40 Torquay

Dear Daddy,

As this letter will only be read after my death, it may seem a somewhat macabre document, but I do not want you to look on it in that way. I have always had a feeling that our stay on earth, that thing we call 'Life', is but a transitory stage in our development and that the dreaded monosyllable 'Death' ought not to indicate anything to be feared. I have had my fling and must now pass on to the next stage, the consummation of all earthly experience. So don't worry about me; I shall be all right.

I would like to pay my tribute to the courage which you and mother have shown, and will continue to show in these tragic times. [They had three serving sons.] It is easy to meet an enemy face to face, and to laugh him to scorn, but the unseen enemies Hardship, Anxiety and Despair are very different problems. You have held the family together as few could have done, and I take off my hat to you.

Now for a bit about myself. You know how I hated the idea of

ὣς ὁ μὲν ἔνθ'
ἀπόλωλε, φίλοισι δὲ
κήδέ ὀπίσσω πᾶσιν,
ἐμοὶ δὲ μάλιστα,
τετεύχαται.

Odyssey.

Thus has he fallen yonder,
and to his friends grief
is allotted for the future,
to all, but most of all to me.

24/5/41.

21/8/40

Dear Daddy,

As this letter will only be read after my death it may seem a somewhat macabre document, but I do not want you to look on it in that way. I have always had a feeling that our stay on earth, that thing which we call 'Life', is but a transitory stage in our development, and that the dreaded monosyllable 'Death' ought not to indicate anything to be feared. I have had my fling, and must now pass on to the next stage, the consummation of all earthly experience. So don't worry about me; I shall be all right.

I would like to pay tribute to the courage which you and mother have shown, and will continue to show in these tragic times. It is easy to meet an enemy face to face, and to keep him to scorn, but the unseen enemies, Hardship, Anxiety and Despair are a very different problem. You have both the family together as few could have done, and I take off my hat to you,

an ideal pair in our relations to each other.

All I can do now is to voice my faith that this war will end in victory, and that you will have many years before you in which to resume a normal civil life. Good luck to you!

Pat.

War, and that hate will remain with me for ever. What has kept me going is the spiritual force to be derived from Music, its reflection of my feelings, and the power it has to uplift the soul above earthly things. Mark [who was lost at sea in January 1942] has the same experiences as I have in this though his medium of encouragement is Poetry. Now I am off to the source of Music, and can fulfil the vague longings of my soul in becoming part of the fountain whence all good comes. I have no belief in a personal God, but I *do* believe most strongly in a spiritual force which was the source of our being, and which will be our ultimate goal. If there is anything worth fighting for, it is the right to follow our own paths to this goal and to prevent our children from having their souls sterilised by Nazi doctrines. The most horrible aspect of Nazism is its system of education, of driving in instead of leading out, and of putting State above all things spiritual. And so I have been fighting.

All I can do now is to voice my faith that this war will end in victory, and that you will have many years before you in which to resume normal civil life. Good luck to you!

Knowing his feelings about fighting offered Flora some comfort; at least he had been spared something: 'I think it would have destroyed him to drop bombs on people, so it was probably the best thing for him. It meant he didn't live to be disillusioned by the war. No one was the same again, but he was saved all that, spared from fighting Hitler.'

Six months later, the family was told that Mick's aeroplane had been on a special mission. 'He had been flying a Blenheim, for which there would have been no hope in daylight. We thought he might have had a chance to make a forced landing. We didn't have anything, we hadn't ended his life, there was no funeral. It was terrible for my mother because she only wanted sons. I became so irrational in my deep sorrow. You never get over it, I can cry about it now. It was probably during one of those anguished times that I threw away all the letters he wrote me. Even now I think – suppose he had lost his memory, or they find the body, it's one of my nightmares. For the whole of the war we thought he might turn up so we never grieved properly.'

It didn't end there. In six months, Flora had lost another brother,

Mark. 'I had a breakdown when Mick was missing. He was the closest person to me ever. Three days into a new job in the Lake District Father sent me a telegram saying that Mark was missing believed killed. He'd tried to take Mick's place and written to me in the term I'd been ill and hadn't worked. When my father was nearing the end of his life he wrote and said, "I'm just a bitter old man."

'It was ghastly for my brother Bill who had also joined up and was on the *Ark Royal*. He was shattered by the war. He was on the *Ark Royal* when she was torpedoed. When she was being towed into Gibraltar, before the "abandon ship" was sounded he knew that if she sank he would go down with her as he was stationed in the hospital. He also suffered appalling guilt that he'd survived when Mick and Mark hadn't. It was awful when Bill came back, I remember feeling he was the wrong one, I didn't want him. Bill had said to my parents that when the war was over he would get married and give them three sons. He finally married at fifty-three, to a much younger girl, and they have three wonderful sons.'

There was one final letter from Mick to his parents written only weeks before his death, anticipating and coming to terms with it concomitantly. The reader can sense the freedom, the release as the writer relives the physical experience of soaring through the clouds and seeing the world below from above, literally and metaphorically. Flying made it possible for Mick to contemplate death fearlessly, almost with exuberance, to embrace it without regret. It robbed him of his life, but if it hadn't been for the war, he would never have experienced the pleasure of it.

7/5/41 Wattisham

Dear Mother and Daddy,

You now know that you will not be seeing me anymore, and perhaps the knowledge is better than the months of uncertainty which you have been through. There are one or two things which I should like you to know, and which I have been too shy to let you know in person.

Firstly let me say how splendid you both have been during this terrible war. Neither of you have shown how hard things must have been, and when peace comes this will serve to knit the family together as it should always have been knit. As a family we are terribly afraid of showing our feelings, but war has uncovered unsuspected layers of affection beneath the crust of gentlemanly reserve.

Secondly I would like to thank you both for what you have done for me personally. Nothing has been too much trouble, and I have appreciated this to the full, even if I have been unable to show my appreciation.

Finally a word of comfort. You both know how I have hated this war, and dreaded the thought of it all my life. It has, however, done this for me. It has shown me new realms where man is free from earthly restrictions and conventions; where he can be himself playing hide and seek with the clouds, or watching a strangely silent world beneath, rolling quietly on, touched only by vague unsubstantial shadows moving placidly but unrelenting across its surface. So please don't pity me for the price I have had to pay for this experience. This price is incalculable, but it may just as well be incalculably small as incalculably large, so why worry?

There is only one thing to add. Good luck to you all!

ROSEMARY GARVEY
&
PETER PRITCHARD

Rosemary Garvey's brother Peter Pritchard was in the RAF in Bomber Command until his death during the Second World War. He was born on 26 September 1921, and after leaving school in July 1939, began his RAF training in October and completed it in August 1940. As Rosemary remembers it the RAF in 1940–41 was very different from the Army or the Navy: 'They lived in quite different circumstances. They were in and out of real life all the time. Someone would write a note to a friend on a Thursday, making a date for Saturday, and then one of them would go missing on Friday. Of course anyone on operations knew in his heart that each note might be his last, but it happened so often, that each one of them had to sublimate that thought.'

Looking back over Peter's letters, written both to his sister and to his closest friend John Davey, Rosemary realized 'that not one of them was written with any idea that it was to be the last. This was probably peculiar to the RAF – those in other services would go off for months or years in a ship, or to a war zone far away, they would say goodbye to loved ones and the separation was complete. I expect these people (which included airmen actually based in some distant land), quite cut off and quite lonely, were more likely to write a letter which is consciously a last one, or which they think may be, before going into an attack or out on a mission, or during some long boring spell of inactivity, wanting or needing to put their thoughts into words for their loved ones.'

It is clear, too, that there is a qualitative difference, at least for airmen, between letters written during the early period of the war when the chances of survival were, and were recognized to be, low (there were too few planes and too few pilots and an enemy who appeared to be invincible), and those written later, when the Allies had the weapons they needed and were more confident. 'Not that I have many later letters, but I remember the change in tone (belief in victory, impatience with the long duration, occasional unease about what your own side might be asked to do, such as mass bombing of German cities). It is easier to be single-minded about war when you have your back to the wall.'

Rosemary's brother Peter and his great friend John Davey began their training together, Peter going to Bomber Command, John to Fighter Command. On 13 August 1940, Peter wrote to John. He never received the letter; he was killed on 11 August. John's mother sent the letter back to Peter:

R.A.F. Station
Upper Heyford
Oxford
Telephone – Bicester 197

13/8/40

My Dear John –

We're more or less installed in the above dump or joint which, relatively speaking, is not too bad. There is no hot water, the food is excellent and I and a selection of earwigs sleep together in a hut on a cast-iron bed with a concrete pillow. Up to date we've been navigating around the British Isles in Ansons – horrible things. One trip took us down to Cornwall and out into the Atlantic. On another we flew across Wales up to the Isle of Man and then up to Scotland. We had supper at Aldegrove in N. Ireland and flew back from there at night. We do a goodish amount of night flying and in particular night x-countrys. At the moment we are flying Ansons for a week before going on to Hampdens. Ansons, by the way, are phenomenal aircraft. They stall at about forty and behave like a Tiger Moth. The cockpit lay-out is appalling and we all think with affection of the Oxford in that respect. I've more or less learnt the Hampden cockpit by heart. Rather like an organ; and with luck we will soon be flying the things.

I heard rumours that you and Tim Elkington shot Cranwell up and got hauled up by Wood. Good show. We also heard that Phillips is now on Whitleys because he couldn't formate in a Spitfire. The man will probably go off his head with rage.

I got a letter from brother Jackson. He and Slatter are flying Wellingtons which they seem to like. Whatley, W. Smith, Gilbert, Haigh and one or two others are flying Hudsons and Beauforts.

Have you been participating in any of these field-days off the coasts of England? It's high time you were slaughtering Huns, my boy.

Herefords incidentally are bloody.

Let me know your scandal when you have an interval during the Battle of Britain.

Yours ever –
Peter

PS Give my love to Comrade Elkington

15 Milverton Crescent
Tel 1059 Leamington

August 30th 1940

Dear Mr. Pritchard,

I think a letter from 'Peter' to John is from you – and on the off chance I write this line. I could tell you more of our darling John's death when I know it is you – and that this finds a home – it still seems like a dream – He had been hit in the fight on Sun. a.m. 11th ... and made a forced landing behind Sandown I.O.W. The field was small and an insignificant hedge he apparently hoped to negotiate (– they say his wings would have topped it –) proved to be a hedge on a bank – 3 to 4 feet high – the impact with the bank killed him instantaneously ...

He was buried with service honours – near the spot – on 15th.

Best of luck and God bless you!

Yours sincerely,
Elise Davey
(John's mother)

Mrs Davey's letter to Peter telling him of John's death marked the beginning of a correspondence which was to last until Peter, too, was killed. He wrote to her on 2 September, telling her of the importance of their friendship, of John's exceptional qualities as a human being, and of the quiet heroism that Peter believed John possessed.

R.A.F. Station,
Upper Heyford,
Oxford
Telephone – Bicester 197

2/9/40

Dear Mrs. Davey,

It was kind of you to write to me and I know how you must feel having lost so fine a son. He was my best friend and I shall never look back on the times we had together with anything but pleasure and pride to think that he was my friend.

The letter you mentioned was from me. I was in London this weekend and intended to ring John up when I saw his name in the casualty list.

I think he was one of the most exceptional people I have ever known. He could talk with authority on any subject, from shooting to religion, from Rugger to politics. He seemed to have a natural capacity for leadership. I found I automatically turned to him for advice and guidance on all occasions, and it never failed to be good advice.

John loved every minute in the Air Force and as a pilot he had a reputation for more than usual ability. It is hard to try to offer you any consolation, but I think it must fill you with pride to know that John was among those in the fighter squadrons who so far have saved England.

I have only one thing more to say in this letter. If at any time I can do anything which may be of use to any of you, please let me know, for I should like to do nothing better.

Yours sincerely,
Peter Pritchard.

Mrs Davey replied on 4 September, filling Peter in on the details of John's death, the swiftness of it after a mere month serving his squadron, and the beauty of his burial service:

15 Milverton Crescent

Tel. 1059 Leamington

September 4th 1940

Dear Mr. Pritchard,

Your very kind letter about John is a great consolation to us – we
know how much John valued your friendship – you were so to
speak interwoven with his flying career . . . and we all feel we know
you a certain amount.

How swiftly he went . . . and how disappointed he would have
been had he known he was to serve his squadron but for 4 weeks!!
Thank God he is out of reach of disappointment and sorrow! He no
longer must toil on this earth – but has reached his real eternal life
in so short a space . . .

On Sunday 11th Aug. 6 of his squadron and 9 of another set
out on droves of German bombers. The fight took place 1/2 way or
more to the French coast. John was hit. From all accounts his
radiator was leaking – obscuring his windscreen – and he was
emitting white smoke intermittently – a pilot said – He could not
make his base – and suddenly turned at right angles off the course
he was taking, and came over Sandown . . . (observer Corps saw it
all – about 11:30 a.m.) Here he circled a few times – coming in –
let down his undercarriage and made a perfect landing they say in a
field that was all too small – the golf links were studded with
players. The meadows had sprinklings of children playing about
. . . and people on the spot say he chose the only available free
ground. . . . And as I told you it was bound by a small hedge on a
formidable bank – He had been leaning out of his cockpit . . . – the
impact must have killed him immediately – he was thrown out and
under his machine – which blazed for two hours – yet he was not
burnt – his flying kit only scorched. His head was most severely
injured. Sandown made a great fuss of him . . . and praised his skill
in handling his plane under extremely difficult circumstances. A
pilot however – says he might have effected a landing on the beach
– but it is easy to be wise after the event! – the observers thought
he might make a safe landing inland as he tried . . . On Thursday
15th he was buried with full service honours – we all went down –

it was most impressive – and beautiful. A wonderful day – free from raids for the first time for about 10 consecutive days – and we really 'sensed' the wonderful peace and calm in which John is now wrapt.

I'm enclosing you a memorial card of John – possibly you may not wish to retain it? – but I send it on the off chance – I don't know your views on the matter.

We shall often think of you and wish you a very happy and successful time. I shall be glad when the war is over and your risks diminished – we shall remember to pray for your welfare and happiness – now and always knowing how John would wish this.

Thank you again for a beautiful letter.

Yours sincerely,
Elise Davey

On 11 June 1941, nine months after the death of his friend, Peter Pritchard went missing over Germany. Recently, Rosemary found the last letter Peter's girlfriend Joanna wrote to him in a collection of her mother's letters. 'She was his current girlfriend. He had flown over to see her the day he was to set off, in the evening, on his last flight. Having seen him during the day, she wrote to him that very evening, his visit still in her mind, his departure, literally into the clouds, the last sight she would ever have of him.'

Royal Air Force
Mildenhall
Bury St Edmunds
Tel. Mildenhall 2281

11.6.41

My Darling,

It was lovely seeing you today. I feel much better now. Although after you had just gone I felt awful, you seemed to disappear so quickly into the clouds, and left me standing there with an ache in my throat, however I managed to walk back to the mess although my legs didn't seem to function very well. When I got back I didn't know what to do with myself, I felt so restless, I couldn't read and I couldn't sit still so I wandered round and round a small piece of grass chewing my nails. See what a bad effect you have on me?

After tea I was roped in to play tennis. I can't play the game at the best of times, but this evening I was worse than usual, my partner got awfully annoyed with me but I didn't care, I felt too happy, having seen you.

I am writing now in bed, I have just had a lovely hot bath and feel so warm and comfy, I hate to think of you having to fly tonight while I just sleep peacefully in my little bed. It seems so unfair that you R.A.F. people are having to do all the work. I am awfully thrilled about your 3rd stripe, the only trouble is I can't write F's and it is awful having to put F on all your letters, can I promote you to S/? as I like doing S's! But seriously it is a jolly good show.

I hope it won't be long before we can snatch a few more hours together, it just makes life worth living for me. I must go to sleep now.

Goodnight my darling,
From Jo xx

Nine months later, Joanna became engaged to a friend of Peter's. The announcement was sent to the papers, and was put in on 13 March. In fact, her fiancé, Charles, had been killed returning from Germany two days earlier, on 11 March. Joanna, who had kept in touch with Peter's parents, wrote to tell them of this second 'crushing blow', clearly finding it very difficult to cope with:

Royal Air Force
Mildenhall
Bury St Edmunds
Tel: Mildenhall 2281

25.3.42

My Dear Mrs. Pritchard,

I have been meaning to write to you for such a long time, as I have been wondering so much what you have been doing and if you are well – I was going to write such a happy letter, as for several months I have been so happy. Do you remember me mentioning to you Charles Pilkington who was stationed here and knew Peter at Eton? I grew to love him very much and became unofficially engaged to him. We couldn't get married at once because he hadn't finished his operations and partly because he was only 20. However on March 9th his parents and my parents gave their consent and the announcement was sent to the papers. On March 11th Charles was killed when his aircraft crashed a mile from his aerodrome on returning from a trip over Germany.

The announcement of our engagement didn't get into the papers until March 13th. We were so very very happy and so once again I feel as if I've had a crushing blow. This time I am finding it very hard to get up and live again, however I carry on with my work although half of me has been torn away.

I am sure Peter and Charles are together now, we often talked of Peter and as I said I have been meaning to write to you for such a long time. So please if you have time just write and tell me how you are and what news you have of Rosemary.

You would have loved Charles he was so like Peter.

Much love Joanna

Rosemary remembers the post as being very fast, deliveries frequent, and writing being the normal way to keep in touch. 'Peter and people like him spent much time writing to the families of their friends who were killed and their letters were often marvellous, given most of the writers were nineteen or twenty, even the wing commanders and the squadron leaders on whom much of the writing to families fell were usually under twenty-five. Then there were the on-going exchanges and the friendships formed. Peter went on writing to Mrs Davey until he died the following June, Joanna to my mother till long after the war.'

Peter wrote to their mother several times a week. It was something they needed to do. 'Flying people lived under great strain, each morning someone missing at breakfast, and so on, and I reckon they felt most at ease with friends engaged in the same sort of life, not just those flying but everyone on the station, air crew, WAAFS, maintenance, all. They were in it together and interdependent. Several letters talk about the faith in their ground crews, looking after their planes like a nanny and so on. A week's leave was worth having but, as time went by, very short leaves away from the environment were often tense. In conversation, people had to make light of disaster – "silly idiot went and hit a church" – sort of stuff, and this sometimes hit a facetious or callous note. It wasn't, as everyone knew, but it rippled the waters. Telephone calls, except for short practical messages, often induced silence and paralysis. All that apart, letters gave relatives and friends something to hold on to.'

Peter's last letter to his mother has 'no special significance' according to Rosemary; it was a hastily scribbled note written as he rushed off to meet a friend. Rosemary's thoughts on the singular case of the bomber crews were applicable to many, and more personally to her mother when Peter tragically went missing. 'They often went missing, perhaps turned up as POWs, occasionally they escaped or were presumed dead, but there was sometimes no finality till the war was over. This was hard on everyone. My mother went on hoping without hope, until after the war we got a letter from a Danish farmer on whose land Peter had crashed, plus photographs of the funeral taken between the legs of the German guard of honour. The farmer was a member of the Danish Resistance.'

PART III

Last Letters Home

KENNETH
&
PENELOPE STEVENS

On 10 February 1942 Kenneth Stevens was taken prisoner by the Japanese. Unable to get letters out to his wife, Penelope, he kept a diary throughout his time at a prisoner-of-war camp. It is, in effect, his last letter. He was clearly determined to describe the daily life of the camps, the marching, the work, the conditions, and – perhaps more importantly – to look at his past and present life with Pen and his son Christopher, and look forward to their future together.

His last letter to her before the arduous march to a prisoner-of-war camp in the jungle on the Siam-Burma border is written into a new version of his will, fearing that the one he has already given Pen could have gone missing:

Changi
27/4/43

Pen darling,

It has occurred to me that the will I gave you may have gone astray during your adventures, so I am making another one herewith, in view of my departure tomorrow for Heaven knows where.

My financial assets should be as follows:

1. My account with the Chartered Bank, Singapore. This may be about $500 or over $1,000, depending upon whether the firm paid in a cheque for the equivalent of £100 bonus in January 1941. This bonus was promised so if it wasn't paid, ask them for it, referring to Ferdie.
2. Two or three pounds in Lloyds Bank, New Bond Street.
3. About $25 in the P.O. Savings Bank, Singapore.
4. A life insurance policy for $16,000 with the Manufacturers' Life Co. of Singapore. Premiums ($35 monthly) were paid up to the end of March 1941 I believe.
5. A male staff endowment policy of the D.R.C's with the 'Scottish Widows and Orphans Insurance Co.'. I am afraid I am not quite clear as to the rights of this owing to trouble I had over the medical side. But I think you might get £2500 or £3000 from this. Refer to Ferdie.
6. The D.R.C. promised (by a letter from Ferdie – since destroyed)

to pay my salary up to June 1941, after which the matter would be discussed further. Further to this they might make you a special grant in view of the fact that I was so long overdue for leave. I had been out since January 1936 – don't be afraid to ask for anything you can get from them.

7. Army pay from February 15th, 1941 at the rate of $3.68 per day is due to me and, if I am killed, there will be a pension too.

8. *Liabilities*. I owe Mooty $100 (one hundred) and Sinyar Co. $150 (one hundred and fifty). I should also like you to do something for Ah See in the way of a small monthly payment or some such. You will see the amount I want you to pay Mum – I'm afraid it reduces the already small total you will receive but I fear she will be very hard up otherwise. I am not leaving anything to Angela as I know she will get all Mum's property – I know she will understand.

Well darling, I'm afraid it's a poor situation to leave you in. But I do hope you will marry again and *soon*, because you are much too marvellous a person to be left alone. If you make someone else one hundredth part as happy as you have made me, he will be a lucky man.

I have only two wishes about Christopher. I would like him to have two years schooling on the Continent between 17 and 20 so that he can learn the more beautiful side of life instead of becoming as narrow-minded as English education only makes us. The other is that I would like him to grow up in the country, not in a big town. But this depends on your wishes.

I feel so dreary to be writing this in this way but I wanted you to know where we stood financially. Will start scribbling notes in the train tomorrow to show you I really do intend to come out of this alive, and to look after you a little better in future.

All my love for always, darling,
Kenneth

P.S. The witnesses to the will are A. F. Anderson, of F.M.S.V.F. and W.N. /Rothery of S.S.V.F.

But only a few months earlier, in December 1942, Kenneth had had
no idea if Pen had got out of Singapore safely. In fact, he feared she might
be dead. The ship on which she had left, the *Kuala*, had been bombed and
abandoned. In April 1942 he had written in his diary that he believed
Pen had been on board. Despite this, he wrote her a letter in which he
elaborated on his feelings for her and looked back on their pre-war life
together (often with remorse), hardly daring to imagine their future:

It's difficult, my precious, to write to you all the things I would so
much rather say – my great fear always now is that I might be
killed accidentally in a motor smash or in one of our own bombing
raids which will possibly be starting soon – before I have a chance
of seeing you again and telling you how completely wonderful you
were in those days.

When I think of those last two months in Singapore – how first
you had to cope with Mama in her worst moods, then took in
Angela and David, then Monty for her baby and how all the time
you were working so hard at the hospital and yet running the house
like clockwork. And then worst of all when you had to send your
lovely Christopher away and with Mama at that, and with me being
absolutely no help to you, not even right at the end – Oh darling
how can I ever tell you how tremendously I admire your courage
and your steadiness thro' all that terrible time. You know, I think,
how enormously proud I have always been of you being my wife –
that was based on you just being your adorable self, making such a
lovely home for me, having such a wonderful baby, always being so
obviously such a very charming person. So what can I say about you
now when on top of all that you have shown yourself to be so brave
and true to yourself under conditions which undermined the very
strongest and shook so many bigwigs to the ground. You will never
get a medal for it, my darling, and after the war there will be so
many loud and noisy people shouting about what *they* have done
that the real people won't be even heard – will it be enough for you
that at least *I* will have seen and understood the quality that you
showed?

Oh darling, if only it's within my power to make you as happy as you deserve to be.

The future's very frightening, darling – I shall have to start all over again.

The opening pages of Kenneth's diary, which is otherwise written in ink, are a pencilled index of hundreds of recipes that he has then written out in detail in every available margin or corner of every page. It reads like an early edition of *Mrs. Beeton*, with a few touches from the Far East. Pages of very English cakes, devilled fowl legs and oyster patties are written alongside the more exotic Nasi Goreng and Mah Mee. It can hardly have been a pleasurable experience, imagining the joys of home cooking, when the realities were so grimly different. Daily rations were totally inadequate, illness rife, and a large part of every day was spent dreaming about the food the prisoners weren't getting.

March 14 1943

Rations are lower and lower – 400 lbs of veg. and 80 lbs fish are what 200 men have had this week. We now have an 'excellent' fish paste which we make from literally nothing else than heads, tails and backbones ground up and fried with coconut oil!!

By 25 May, a 'hospital' had been opened up, and Kenneth was admitted, staying there until 11 June, but there were almost no medicines, and while still a patient he contracted the violent diarrhoea which is a forerunner of cholera.

I starved myself for five days (in which my total ingoings were four cups of tea!) and managed to get over it but I reduced myself to skin and bone and am as weak as a rat . . . for breakfast ⅓ mess tin browned or semi-burnt rice, lunch ½ tin and dinner ¼ pint meat stew and rice (they kill 2 emaciated bullocks or 'yaks' as the soldiery know them every other day).

But one is always hungry and FOOD occupies all our thoughts – I'm afraid I even write out a daily menu of what I would have at Chancery Hill!

Yet there was some good news. On Sunday 28 March 1943, Kenneth had received word that Christopher and Pen had been reunited:

Nothing matters now that Pen and Christopher are together – it's almost a peaceful world!!

And on 4 April, a letter from Pen got through, dated the previous 22 July, with a photograph of the two of them. On 15 June he wrote a long letter to Pen criticizing and analysing his perceived shortcomings, and reflecting and reminiscing in great detail on their life together, and the plans he wants – if her approval is granted – to come home and realize with her. Despite its reference to the extraordinarily hard and harrowing time he is undergoing, it is never self-pitying, and never dwells on the hideously inhumane conditions to which he is victim. It tells, with quiet courage and dignity, of the dreams that keep him going, and he recognizes the strengths he feels he has not properly acknowledged in his wife Pen before their separation, and in their relationship together.

Tuesday June 15th 1943

Penelope my own darling,

Life has become extremely grim since I last wrote you at Changi. I don't want to talk about it much because I think about you all the time and the sooner I forget this the better. But we are in a rather terrible P.O.W. camp in the jungle on the Siam–Burma border, 192 miles from Ban Pong in Siam and 80 miles from Madmein in Burma. Food's very scarce and medical supplies also and we are coping with cholera, dysentery and beri-beri – we have lost 160-odd men out of 1600 in the first 3 weeks here but things are slightly better now. Getting here was rather an ordeal – 3 weeks of marching thro' the jungle at night, everything having to be carried in our packs. It was the most exhausting business and was undoubtedly the cause of so many deaths here as people had very little resistance left. I developed ulcerated sores on my legs and arms about half way thro' the journey but these were really a blessing in disguise as I went into 'hospital' as soon as we arrived here, so I had a good rest. I was in for 18 days and early on got a bit scared as I developed the early signs of cholera so I starved myself completely for 5 days and managed to get over it. It has left me a bag of bones and very weak but I am still lying up so am alright. I spend the whole time living my life with you both in the past and what I hope for in the future. It was an inspiration for you to send me that photo of you and Christopher – I looked at it for hours on end, although actually Christopher didn't figure so very much in my thoughts – it was nearly all you – I think it was that I needed you so badly. Oh darling, I do so passionately want to come out of this alive to be with you again – I'm sure I'll be such a nicer person and I do want to be able to show you every day of my life how much I appreciate you and all your wonderfulness. I have thought so much of Chancery Hill and what a beautiful home you made of it and how proud I was of it, and of your making a real home out of a Singapore house! It was nice to go to Jorrocks and Mickie's or to Angela's or to Ma's and then come back to our own dear place with thankfulness in my heart that we lived there and not in other people's houses. You have always said that Angela's efficiency frightened you, but did you ever stop to realise how full her house was of domestic crises and rows with the servants and last minute rushes? But your house seemed to run like clockwork – there is only one excuse for not showing my appreciation of your skill more clearly – it is only looking back from this distance that I realise that it was hard work and efficiency on your part that accounted for it. (To be fair to Angela I must admit that you didn't have Victor to cope with!)

In this place, one's mind returns continually and dwells longingly on Food – do you know darling, that when I think of all the dishes I'd like to be having, it is always in Chancery Hill that I think of eating them because they were always much better there than at anyone else's house or at any hotel. I think the only dish I think of elsewhere is Crumbly Cutlets, and I think that is because I don't remember ever having them at home. But when I think of Duck and Cherry Casserole, Scrambled Eggs, Fish Scallops, Chicken Stanley, Kedgeree, Trifle, Summer Pudding, Fruit Fool, Bread & Butter Pudding – all those lovely things were made just perfectly 'right' in my own home.

Then there was the time you had coping with the difficulties of Mama and Monty and her baby, all at the same time as you were working endlessly at the hospital. And of course, above all there was our completely wonderful Christopher Michael and I don't think anyone can deny that there were few babies like him in Malaya. So there you are, darling, as wife, housewife, housekeeper, hostess and mother you were a complete and outstanding success – do you wonder that I feel uncertain as to whether I can ever make up to you for the risks and unhappiness of the last 2 years? By the way, you have also been wonderful in fixing up the insurance policies for yourself and Christopher's education – you know, dearest, that it wasn't slackness on my part that it wasn't done but due to this nonsense about my old heart but still I'm sorry that you have had the trouble of having to do it, I am hoping that either the DRC or the Govt. are giving you money to live on – there were supposed to have been arrangements made when we first went out to Changi as POWs but I doubt if they ever got thro' to England. It's getting dark, sweetie, so I must stop. Loving you so tremendously much *all* the time.

July 4th, Sunday

Did you remember 'Rabbits Happy Month' on July 1st, darling? I did – and I remember, I think that I cheated last year on July 1st and pinned a paper to the mosquito net. Oh dear, I mean 2 years ago – how awful!!

This separation from you is getting worse and worse – I am getting used to all the rest of this beastliness but not being with you is sheer misery that becomes worse every day and week that I am away from you. The only comfort is that you are with your family. – I'm so thankful to have had that news so that I don't have to torture myself with dreading what may be happening to you. I don't deserve to have this enormous relief after having looked after you so carelessly but I have got it and am grateful for it.

The lapse in time between the beginning of this letter and now is due to my tummy having gone back on me again – in mid-June I was moved from the lines up to another bit of the 'hospital' known delicately as 'The Diarrhoea Centre' and I have stayed there ever since. I am well off, as it happens because I am hideously spoilt – our own R.S.M. is in charge and the No. 2 is a Sergeant Judson, a Regular, who has been a second Harold Godwin to me, for some reason or other and I have had everything done for me, including extra tit-bits now and then, and *those* in this place are more precious than rubies.

Sunday July 11th/43. Darling sweetheart, the preceding pages of this letter sound like a reference written for a governess – I'm sorry they are so stilted but I wanted to particularise more about you than just to say, 'Darling, you're completely wonderful', which really sums up the rest.

I've been thinking of you so much today – I do always of course and especially on Sundays (I always think of our quieter Sundays at Chancery Hill, but today I've been letting my mind wander back over any odd moments which seem specially happy even against the background of all my happiness with you.

Do you remember, darling, lunch in that dear little inn when we were motoring up to Dalat? How sunny and fresh the air was and how lovely you looked sitting on the other side of the table with the sunlight on your hair. It was lovely to get away from Saigon, wasn't it?

And then there was breakfast in our sunny room with its big window at the hotel – how lovely it all was with the pine trees down below, instead of our going into that stiff suite in the front. And our dear little 'pension' where we all used to have tea – and walking over to the market in the cold evening wind afterwards – and the first time we had strawberries and cream at that farm. And back in Saigon the excitement of finding that canteen of cutlery, and of choosing our lacquer tables – how sad that all those have gone now. And happy Sunday morning breakfasts (with Nathaniel

Gubbins!) under the flame tree at Tanah Merah – and supper upstairs on Sundays. And the joy of coming home to lunch at Chancery Hill with old Bunchy chuckling on amah's knee and dear old Ah See. And our lovely bedroom, specially after bath time in the evening and when those bedside lamps (I always loved them and do you remember what a last minute purchase they were!) were on – and bicycling and shopping in the tiddler in High St. in the evenings, and the excitement and soul-searching of buying plants – oh darling, there have been some lovely good times to make up for the bad – I only hope they are as precious to you as they are to me. I am not forgetting the times I was so horrid at Dalat, or how dim I used to be at Tanah Merah when I got back from the office or my often drinking too much or my spoiling motoring and sailing for you or what you suffered from Mama or how awful I make your Christmases for you – can you try to forget them darling and remember just the good times? Because I think it is going to be rather important for facing the future for you to feel that I can make you happy. I have thought about it all so carefully this long time but most especially this 2 months I have been in hospital and I have reached a decision that only you can alter if you disapprove. Before I start I must tell you that Ah See, wife and imp are safe and sound and live under the sheltering wing of the Enormous One (who used to call you the 'Voluptuous Pen') – I didn't dare mention this before in case the letter was impounded in Singapore and it might have got him into trouble, but up here it doesn't matter.

I think I shall offer Ah See a trip home with me if he would like it and he might be willing to stay 2 or 3 years with us which I think you would like as much as I. Whatever happens, I shall pension him off – £35 a year would give him $25 a month and he could then afford either not to work or, if he did, he could safely provide for his old age. He stayed at the house to the bitter end – I saw him there on Sat. Feb. 14th and fool that I was, told him that things would improve – we were expecting reinforcements of aircraft from Java on the 16th – anyhow it was good advice as Chinatown was getting an awful battering and the house was untouched. There were troops there – Northumberland Fusiliers –

and they hadn't touched a thing of ours, I threw open our store cupboard to them, and I told Ah See I would be back the next day, but of course never got the chance. Luckily, I gave him $40 (which wasn't mine!) and anyhow he is safe.

Alas! darling, I don't know about Chips – the only moment I have seen Ah See since, we were both in tears and only had a moment to talk about you and were then interrupted by my Nip guard, but it is possible that our darling loopy Chippy is still safe and sound with Ah See.

Now, my most darling, about the future. Any decisions I mention as having been made are, you will know, entirely subject to your views – you are my whole life, past, present and future and as long as I am with you I can do anything.

Firstly, we have finished with the East. However attractive an offer the firm may offer me, I feel that you would prefer starting again humbly at home than our living even in much comfort out here. Now that you are reunited with your family you will know how much more important they are to you than anyone else and that one separation is enough: then there is your health, so much better in a colder climate and the end of your misery from mosquito bites: then there is the appalling experience you passed thro' in getting away from here: and finally of course, Christopher. As far as I am concerned, I feel that all ties with this country have been so brutally severed that now is the time to make a clean break before I get too old. Also I simply yearn for England with you – it will be such a lovely place. And then it is going to take 18 months to 2 years for me to build myself up to proper strength again after the last 2 months and the time we still have to do.

If we are agreed on this point, the question of making a living arises. Darling, would you like to be a Baker's wife? A man I have become very friendly with since capitulation – TAM INNES-KER – and I have worked out all the provisional details of a scheme to buy up a small bakery at ACLE in Norfolk – a village a few miles from both Norwich and Yarmouth. It is a few hundred yards from the river Bure which is a big summer boating river and we intend starting a tea-garden to cater for this traffic over and above the bread and confectionery round of the bakery. In Yarmouth we intend to run a beach coffee stall in the season to provide cakes, buns, sausage rolls and curry-puffs then later something for bathers and beach-loungers. And in the winter we want to build up a luxury cake business in Norwich – you know one of my aunts ran a Park Lane cake shop and she will be able to put us up to the ways of the luxury trade.

That is just the broad outline of the scheme, but we have worked out the smaller details as to capital costs, expenditure, staff etc., as well as one can and we have met in this camp many Suffolk and Norfolk men who know the bakery business in these parts and have given us good advice. The reason we have chosen Acle is that it is close to where Tam will be living and also he knows the local squire very well and he owns almost everything round Acle and consequently his influence is going to be valuable but there are several other villages close if Acle proves to be unsuitable. I intend living either over the bakery or in a nearby cottage and hope you will divide your time between there and Ilkley – that is for the first 3 months or so. We shall be installing a good master baker and will be supervising the distribution side of the business and arranging to have the tea garden built. Once the thing is going we can look round for somewhere suited to our own living requirements – personally I think Suffolk is likely to be less bleak than Norfolk, and it will not be very far from Ilkley.

Does it sound awful to you in this brief bald form? I hope not, sweetheart, because I hope your genius for home-making will find happiness in fixing up a cottage in designing, decorating, and building the tea garden at the river's edge and in looking for and making a permanent home for us. The disadvantages are that we shall be very hard up to start with, but on the other hand we shall be living in the country and above all shall be working for ourselves. Tam is a complete dear and I think you will love him – I don't know his wife (at home) but hear she is very quiet and nice.

If the whole thing proves a flop which we think to be most unlikely – at least we shall have lived in a healthy place and will have an interesting life for a bit and a lot of fun. Also darling you will have had all the cherry cakes you want!

The full development of the scheme may take anything up to 2 years as we don't want to go in too deep financially at the beginning and also Tam and I – if things go well – will have to take a bakery course ourselves to know the business thoroughly. I shall, also, probably do 3 months apprenticeship at a big confectioners and tea shop at Kingston, where I have an entree. What share you take in all this is, of course, up to you but I hope it will be an active one – to see you and be with you everyday is all I want but apart from that I think our problems will be worthy of your organising abilities.

You said in your letter that you had been planning for the future but that, poor sweet, is now a year ago! I do hope anyway that your plans mean England. I think of you and me on a June day watching Christopher knee-deep in a field of buttercups and daisies and sorrel. I think of us walking on a bright October morning with the beech trees glowing copper: I think of cold, wet November and our own fireside: of crocuses and snowdrops, and lilac of the Lake District and Devonshire, of Hampshire heaths, of Surrey commons, of Dorset villages – oh darling there is all that wealth of beauty to be seen with you – and I hope that you will still like me enough to get out of life with me just part of what life with you means to me? And there is the Continent to explore with you – in a humble way seeing the real people and staying in the small places and finding life very wonderful. If we can make a success of working for ourselves we are our own masters and can follow our own wishes. If only I can be nice enough for you to love me I feel there is so much we can make out of life – but I do also feel that if I had been more thoughtful for you during our life in Singapore, it would be easier for you. Oh Pen, I love you so – all I want in the world is to see you happy and to feel that I am doing something towards it. If only this long time apart will enable you to forget my faults, and start again showing you what loving you and realising you and appreciating you can mean – well, I've learnt and am still learning my lesson about you – that I have been the luckiest man in the world and hope and pray to be so again.

All my love, my very dearest sweet.
Kenneth.

Between writing this letter and the end of July, Kenneth's diary notes, alongside his own relapse and return to the diarrhoea hospital, the various deaths that he witnessed there:

Sunday July 18th 1943
Seeing 8 men die in the first 36 hours really shook me –

July 25th
3 more gone and 1 last week.
I myself am much better but appallingly weak – can't get up from the knees-bend without a support.

His physical weakness was echoed by great emotional distress when he lost his wedding ring while washing. It had become too loose. Yet a few days' later, on Sunday 1 August, he is jubilant. A friend looking at a drain running through the hut found his ring: 'am absolutely overjoyed'. He is also receiving an extra ration as his legs have given way:

2 more friends gone – it has worried me, especially as I have been having palpitations . . . Harold and the cookery recipes have been an unfailing comfort and interest. An 'extra diet' on Friday night (to which I don't think I was really entitled) was some very diluted but completely heavenly hot, sweet milk!!

This was Kenneth's last entry. On 12 August, his friend and prospective business partner Tam Innes Ker continues:

Ken died at about 8pm on Aug. 10th having relapsed into a coma around about midday. Sgt. Judson and Eddie Woods who were on duty tell me he just drifted quietly away with a smile on his face and was never in any pain . . . Ken's passing has been felt very deeply by all the volunteers and others who knew him, they all had watched the magnificent fight he had put up from the terrible

ulcers he arrived with to the last final struggle against exhaustion, for that is what he really died of.

Kenneth's son Christopher (Kit) remembers the day his mother Pen learnt of his death. He was four, and remembers feeling the tension in the house in Ilkley when his mother came in and saw the letter waiting for her on a plate. As she burst into tears he was carried out, and doesn't remember anything for the next two years. Another year went by and then a letter came from a stranger, a woman who wrote saying that her son, who had had a nervous breakdown on his return from prisoner-of-war camp, had brought back Kenneth's diary with him. It came in the post soon after and as Pen read it, she was moved to tears. Even today, Kit finds it difficult to read his father's diary.

MYRA FORREST,
BETTY KELLY &
GWYN WILLIAMS

I.G. Williams
Submarine Usk

18.4.41

Dearest Betty,

Betty my darling, I think that you won't mind me calling you that for the last time.

As I expect by now my sister has informed you that I have died in fighting for our and other countries, but I may say darling that my last thoughts were of my family and you, and I love you while there is a breath in my body.

I take this the last opportunity of wishing you the happiest marriage which is possible for two people to have and only wish that it was I. Also give my wishes for a happy and long life to your mother, father and all your friends and relations, and with these few last words I close wishing you all the very best.

Your most loving friend,
Gwyn

Gwyn Williams wrote this letter to his sweetheart Betty the day before he left Malta on H.M. Submarine *Usk*. Six days later, on 25 April, it struck a mine off Cape Ben and Gwyn was lost with all his comrades. Betty brought the letter round to Gwyn's parents when she received it, and they kept it until their death in 1972. It was left to Gwyn's sister Myra who has treasured it ever since. It was kept in her father's well-worn wallet in a corner of his old bureau. At first she could not bring herself to look at it; she would take it out of the bureau, touch it and put it back again.

Ten years ago, when she was trying to get Gwyn's papers in order for her children, she finally summoned up the courage to read it. 'There is nothing else tangible to say he's ever lived except me. He has no grave but the sea. He always said he'd write to me if he got into particular danger, and I've got a feeling he did. It was as though he'd anticipated the end, because on his last leave he gave me a list of people who he asked me to send letters to, informing them of his death if it were to happen.

I. G. Williams. A.B.
Submarine Usk.

18. 4. 41

Dearest Betty,

Betty - my darling.
I think that you wont mind me
calling you that for the last time,
as I expect by now my sister as
informed you that I have died in
fighting for our & other countries, but
I may say darling that my last thoughts
were of my family & you, & I love
you while there is breath in my body.
I take this - the last.
opportunity of wishing you the happiest
married which it is possible for two
people to have. & only wish that it
was I. Also give my wishes for a
happy & long life to your Mother
Father, & all your friends & relations,
& with these few last words I close
wishing you all the very best,
Your most Loving Friend
Gwyn.

xx xx c x x
x x xx x x

'The day it happened, my parents went to an operatic show, and my mother was enjoying it when suddenly she had a horrid feeling, and said to my father "Let's go." It was the very day it happened, and it was as if someone had struck her dead, she knew something had happened.

'I remember the day the letter arrived saying Gwyn was missing. The postman whistled and knocked on the door. I answered it. "Here you are, love, your call-up for the Wrens," he said. But I knew it wasn't, it was from the Admiralty. I thought, I can't give this to my mother. I stood on the doorstep for ages, until she eventually called out, "Are you there? Is there a letter?" "It's not for me," I said, as I opened it and gave it to her. The washing lady was there, so it must have been a Monday.'

There was no conclusive news about Gwyn for another four and a half years, until November 1945, when the official confirmation arrived. 'At the time I didn't believe it, I went everywhere trying to find out what had happened to him. We still hoped. Perhaps he had lost his memory, or was in a prisoner-of-war camp.'

As children Myra and Gwyn were extremely close. They often cycled down to the Mumbles together, and if Gwyn met a girl down there, Myra would cycle back on her own. Myra describes them as a double-act. 'When we were little he always read to me, we were in the same bedroom and he would read me stories of all the old naval heroes. He'd say, "When I'm older I'm going to sea, we'll run away and go together." He instilled a love of reading in me. I still think of him. Most days he comes to mind, not in a morbid way.

'I remember going down to tell my aunt he'd gone missing. I got on and off the bus, and the sun was shining on the hill, and I remember thinking he'll never see this again if he doesn't come back. Our last walk together was from home to Neath Station. He gave me the list of people to inform, saying he mightn't come back, and then he said it was necessary to defeat Hitler, and that before the war was over some would have to die.'

As the years passed, Myra wondered what had become of Betty, Gwyn's girlfriend, of whom she had heard nothing since she had brought the letter to Myra's parents in 1941. 'Had she married? Had she had a happy life? And where was she now? I had been wondering how I could get in touch with her. I only knew one person in Port Talbot, my friend Eunice, who had recently come to visit me. I mentioned it to her and asked her if she had any ideas. That set off an amazing course of events. I mentioned Betty's old address which rang a bell with Eunice who checked the deeds of her house and there was the name of Betty's father. Eunice's house is built on the very same spot as Betty's old home! Eunice and her husband had bought the land on which had stood three cottages and their house is built on the same site. Unbelievable.'

Eunice traced Betty's new address from some of the older residents, and found out that Betty had married, had two grown-up children and was living in Essex. Myra wrote to her, and immediately had a telephone call back. The two of them met up in Myra's house in Neath two years ago, fifty-one years after they had last seen one another.

Betty remembers her first meeting with Gwyn. They were in the local swimming baths one Thursday afternoon – the only afternoon her friend had off. Betty was standing on the edge when someone pushed her in. 'Gwyn jumped in to save me, although I didn't need saving.'

They knew each other for about a year before Gwyn was killed. Betty answered every letter he wrote to her, and saw him when he came home on his two leaves. They corresponded more often than they met, as did so many other couples at the time. Betty remembers going to meet Gwyn's parents. 'People didn't go to each other's houses in those days. I was a little bit frightened. Gwyn then seemed to feel that was it, it was the big romance. He bought me a wrist-watch and I said I couldn't accept it, but he insisted. I wore it until my daughter was eleven or twelve. He wanted to get engaged, but I didn't want to be rushed. I was young, only seventeen, and things weren't certain. The last but one letter I got from him was written when he was on leave, so it was uncensored, and he said he was going on a dangerous trip, so it might be the last one I'd get. My father warned me not to tell his parents about it, if I'd had a letter like that now I'd have thought deeply about it, but I was a child, it was all a big adventure. The next thing I got was the letter that Myra has got now, his last.

'I said to Gwyn I felt too young to get tied down, I hadn't lived. I'd said to him, "Let's talk about it on your next leave", but there never was one. He was a very nice boy, he deserved someone good. I was getting ready to go to work in the morning when the letter arrived. I took it off the postman and didn't read it until I got to work. They sent me home. I hung on to it for a while till his parents had heard he'd been killed, then

I gave it to them. I thought, if that's his last letter home, it will be treasured by his parents more than me. At seventeen or eighteen I had my whole life in front of me. Myra's mother told me he thought the world of me, which made me feel very guilty. I was very upset when he died, but death got to be something you lived with, just another thing, and you just got up and felt happy to be alive the next day.

'When Myra's letter came from Neath two years ago I couldn't believe it after fifty years. When I went to see her, we talked about the first time I went round to her home. I remember thinking the same then as I had in 1941, what a waste. I still say it was a waste that he had to go like that so young.'

BETTY GIBBS &
STAN HOWARD

In 1941, when Betty Gibbs was sixteen, she was working in a men's shop in the High Street in Greys, Essex. She worked with Gwen, with whom she became friendly, and they used to spend weekends together. After work on Saturdays they would go to the Working Men's Club in West Thurrock for 'a bit of fun; dancing, singing, and the best ankle competition'. On Sundays 'after the pictures, we would rush home to listen to Vera Lynn at nine o'clock on the wireless'. Betty met Stan Howard, Gwen's brother, on one of these weekends. He was nineteen (three years her senior) and worked at the Tunnel Cement Works. They started courting and after a year (Stan was twenty) he joined up. It was 1942. Stan was an air-gunner with the RAF. On leave, Stan and Betty would go cycling or to the pictures, and on Saturday nights they ended up at 'the Club'.

They wrote to each other for two years – the letters were 'newsy and friendly'. 'Stan knew I went to the Club on Saturdays, he also knew that I met lots of boys at the shop where I worked, because we sold stripes and regimental badges and all sorts to do with the forces. So although we were courting, I was still having a bit of fun and I still went out a bit when he was away.'

In July 1944, Betty, now nineteen, was called up and sent to work at the Government Training Centre at Letchworth. She was in the electrical welding department. In August, she and Stan had leave at the same time. 'This leave, Stan was a bit different. A bit more serious. I liked him but didn't find it easy to be endearing, in fact I found it hard to put into words my affection. He had a nice face but it was troubled with acne. He spent pounds on his acne. He was tall, over six feet, and distinguished-looking – he looked like a man, he wasn't cissified in any way. His face was open, friendly and impish. I had refused to go to bed with him. I wanted to walk up to the altar with a white dress and not give in before I was married. A white dress symbolizes purity – I didn't want to let my mum down. Anyway, if I'd got a baby before I was married, I would have ended up in the workhouse. My mum and dad took me aside while I was courting Stan and told me they didn't want me to get into any "bothers" so I promised I wouldn't.

'In about the second week of August, Stan and I were together. It was the evening and we were in the orchard opposite my parents' house. I was working away from home, he was doing very frightening missions and our leave was ending. I started to cry. Stan said: "You're crying, you love me, why don't we get engaged?" He'd asked me before – I'd always refused. This time I said all right.'

Betty went back to Letchworth. Stan returned to Bracknell where he was based. On 10 September 1944, a month after their engagement, Betty received the following letter; and although she had received many letters from Stan previously, this letter was different. 'At the time when I read it, it touched me. I thought he was a silly old thing. I think he wanted to really press it home how much he thought of me. Or maybe because his work was getting more dangerous, he had a sort of premonition and wanted to let out his feelings for me . . . he was scared. So this letter was special and was a "real love letter".'

My Darling Sweetheart,

Just a few lines hoping to hear that your OK and happy. I'm OK, darling, only I've nothing to write about, so I'm writing my first love letter to you, give a man room, here goes. What wouldn't I give now darling, just to see that expression in your eyes when you look at me. Perhaps you don't know it sweet but I've seen them sparkle and shine when I've come home on leave. Although you've never said a lot of sweet things or endearing words, your eyes have spoken volumes. We've been terribly happy during our three years together, but it is nothing compared to the happiness that will be ours in the future.

Day in and day out, I'm thinking of you darling, picturing you as I left you, wondering what changes I'll find when I see you again. Will you do your hair the same, will your face light up just as wonderfully when you're happy? I'm sure it will, little thing, I know that I love every inch of you sweet. Once this darn war is over, and we can be together again for always, we are going to be the two most happiest people on earth. I love you so much my darling, and will concentrate my whole life in fulfilling your dreams. Your loving sweetheart

Stan
XXXXXXX

$\frac{1}{x}$

Turweston.
Wed. 10th.
Sept. 1944

My Darling Sweetheart,

just a few lines
hoping to hear that you're O.K. & happy.
I'm O.K darling, only I've nothing to
write about, so I'm writing my first love
letter to you, give a man room here goes.
What wouldn't I give now darling, just
to see that expression in your eyes
when you look at me. Perhaps you don't
know it sweet, but I've seen them
sparkle & shine when I've come home on
leave. Although you've never said a
lot of sweet things or endearing words
your eyes have spoken volumes.
We've been terribly happy during our

3 yrs together darling, but it is nothing compared to the happiness that will be ours in the future.

Day in and day out, I'm thinking of you darling, picturing you as I left you, wondering what changes I'll find when I see you again. Will you do your hair the same, will your face light up just as wonderfully when you're happy? I'm sure it will, little thing I know but I love every inch of you sweet. Once this darn war is over, and we can be together again for always, we are going to be the two most happiest people on earth. I love you so much my darling, and will concentrate my whole life in fulfilling your dreams.

Your loving Sweetheart

Stan xxxxixxxx

Well Darling, that doesn't read too badly. All I'm waiting for now is your letter to tell me I'm getting too sentimental again. Well at heart I guess I am a bit soft, only at heart mind you sweet. You'd better take extra special care of that letter, first one of its kind, you may want to read it again one of these days, when you get a bit fed up, frame it after the war . . .

On 27 September 1944, Betty was called into the welfare office at work. She was told that Stan had been killed. 'I was dumbfounded. I couldn't believe it. I had just got engaged. I had just received his first love letter and now his last. I was devastated.'

Stan Howard, who had been on bombing missions over Cologne, and survived, did not die in action. Stan was killed when 'his plane collapsed and came down in a field next to the aerodrome in Bracknell'.

Four months later Betty met Sydney Pagdin, whom she later married.

PART IV

No Goodbyes

GWENYTH & LAURIE STOCKWELL

Laurie Stockwell met Gwenyth Crow when they were at school. He went to the boys' grammar at Hampton, she to the girls' at Twickenham. Both were very keen swimmers. Gwenyth was even put up for the Olympics, but her father wouldn't let her try for them. They had other boyfriends and girlfriends while they were growing up, but not long after leaving school, in 1939, they decided to get married. 'We got married in Oxford, very much against our parents' wishes. His parents were horrified, mine gave their consent unwillingly. We had dinner at the Randolph afterwards with all our RAF friends, everyone got very drunk.'

Laurie had only gone into the RAF at the end of 1939 to do his training. He had volunteered in 1938, but because he was a civil servant he wasn't released until 1939. Gwenyth stayed at home with her parents to begin with, but once Laurie became a flying instructor, they rented a house in Shawbury in Shropshire. 'We had an incredible life, in the heart of the country, but with a wonderful social life. We met lots of young people, dined in the mess, danced, and certainly didn't realize there was a food shortage. I was twenty, Laurie was twenty-two.'

In the middle of 1942 their social life and their life together came to an abrupt end. Laurie volunteered for Bomber Command. Wives were not permitted to live within a thirty-mile radius of where their husbands were stationed. Gwen went back to her parents.

Laurie and Gwen hated being apart. In one undated letter, when he was still training, he wrote telling her how lonely life was without her:

Thank you for the pullover which is also a great success. Thank you for marrying me. No, I'm not going mad, I just feel like thanking you for everything. You have made life so very much happier for me knowing that you are by my side always.

I've been feeling very sad lately however. Spring is showing signs of breaking forth and it has made the empty space feel even emptier, the space, of course is the one you usually take up . . .

'He wanted to get into Pathfinders. Everyone knew it was a one-way ticket. Why do men do these things? I can remember now his excitement, but it was the end of the world for me, my heart was in my boots. I tried not to show it. Well, you can imagine what I thought. Only the *crème de la crème* were accepted. They were all volunteers. He was aware after each leave that we might never see each other again, but I never tried to dissuade him.'

Laurie joined at the beginning of December 1942. 'The only way I knew whether Laurie was on "ops" on Bomber Command was that they were always given a pint of milk for dinner the night before, and he would write and tell me when he'd had milk.'

On the night of 17 January 1943 Laurie flew out on a bombing raid over Berlin. By the following morning he had been reported missing. Gwen was eight months pregnant. The next day a letter came from his commanding officer.

> R.A.F., Station Wigsley,
> Nr. Newark,
> Nottinghamshire.
>
> 18th January 1943.

Mrs. G. H. Stockwell,
87, Fairfax Road,
Teddington,
Middlesex.

Dear Mrs. Stockwell,

It is with regret that I have to corroborate my telegram concerning your husband who is missing from an operation on the night of the 17th–18th January 1943.

Your husband was one of our most reliable and popular Officers, and his absence will be greatly felt by his fellow Officers.

If I receive any further information, you can be assured that I will let you know immediately.

Yours very sincerely,
Group Captain, Commanding,
R.A.F., Station Wigsley.

Five months later another letter came from the Air Ministry:

> Air Ministry
> (Casualty Branch)
> 73–77 Oxford Street
> W1
>
> 29 May 1943

Madam,

I am directed to refer to a letter from this Department dated 24th January 1943, and to inform you with regret that no news has been received of your husband, Flying Officer Laurence Edwin Stockwell, since he was reported missing on the night of 17th/18th January 1943.

The detailed report from his Squadron states that his aircraft set out at 4.27 p.m. to attack an objective at Berlin. At 9.52 p.m. its approximate position was estimated to be in the vicinity of Utrecht, Holland, and at 10.20 p.m. its position was off the west coast of Holland. No news of it or of any of its occupants has since become available from any source.

In view of the time which has elapsed it is felt that there can now be little hope that your husband is alive, but action to presume his death will not be taken until at least six months from the date on which he was reported missing. Such action would then be for official purposes only, and a further letter would be addressed to you before it was taken.

I am to express the Department's deep sympathy with you in your great anxiety, and to assure you that enquiries are continuing through the International Red Cross Committee and any news later received will be immediately passed to you.

I am, Madam,
Your obedient Servant

Gwen remembers the day the telegram arrived: 'My mother was away and my father was at work. I took the dog out for a walk. When I returned, the telegram was on the mat. The Pathfinders always went ahead on any mission, and stayed the longest over the target to protect the other planes. He had got to Berlin, but I later found out the mission had been totally abortive, they had bombed the suburbs and missed the target.

'We were so close there was nothing else I could do but encourage him, but what I really wanted to say was "What about our unborn baby?" He was thrilled about my being pregnant, I knew it was going to be a girl. Laurie had come to the doctor with me on his last leave, and the doctor had turned to him and said, "Don't worry, old chap, I'll look after her." And he did. It was my saving I think. I was determined from the moment I heard about Laurie that it wasn't going to affect the baby. Everyone else thought she'd come on January 19th, she didn't, she came on February 23rd. Both our parents were fantastically supportive.'

Gwen had written to Laurie every day, sometimes twice a day. 'I wanted to keep him in touch with home, however mundane it was. Our letters were an anchor. They were the most important thing in one's life at the time, we just waited for the postman. All my letters to him came back after he was missing. I burnt them all, they were such drivel.'

Laurie had written whenever he could, but it was impossible to write every day if you were in Pathfinders. His last letter arrived two days after he was killed.

Officers' Mess
Royal Air Force
Wigsley
Newark
Notts

15-1-43

Tel: Spalford 241

Gwen Darling,

Please forgive me for not writing these last two days, there is no excuse whatsoever, I've just been a bit browned off, that's all, but as that feeling has passed, everything is O.K. As two of your letters arrived together today, one saying about your fears a few days ago and the other about mother telling you that you should not have told me, and also that it was a false alarm, I was quite happy about things, but please take no notice of mother and tell me everything for I feel much happier if I know what is going on.

The nursery furniture looks quite good. I'd try and get what you can of it. Please forgive me for a terribly short note.

By the way one item of news, or two rather. First I have at last had a receipt from Heyford after threatening to stop payment of the cheque and secondly, we also get a pint of milk nowadays, a glass at breakfast and one at tea.

All my love Darling,
Yours always,
Laurie

However, Laurie had also written Gwen a letter early in 1942 which is, in sentiment and intent, very much a last letter. It is the one that Gwen has treasured most. Laurie had said he would be a conscientious objector before the war; he had cried at the time of saying it at the mere thought of war. This letter synthesizes her feelings about all that he held dear and important. Gwen says that she knew every sentiment in it before she got it: 'I knew anyway, knew exactly how he thought, and he me, it was one of those incredible things we had from childhood. The neighbours used to say, "It's all wrong that those two should be parted." He didn't accept anything. It seems like it's written by someone young because it's so optimistic. Knowing what one knows now, it would be so difficult to write back to it now.'

Sunday

My Darling,

When I was walking back from Heyford Station yesterday, I realised how little I appreciated the beauty of the countryside, how little I seemed to take interest, and on realising that I stopped in the road and looked about me, and for the first time noticed how lovely everything is about here. Having found that out I tried to fathom the question of why I hadn't noticed it before, why I wasn't taking my usual interest in the countryside, for although I'm not of a

poetic nature or anything like it, I feel that I've always taken quite
a lot of interest in my surroundings, I loved the Isle of Wight and
all the places of natural beauty, especially St. Martha's which holds
such wonderful memories for me. And I came to these conclusions.
Firstly, this beastly war. War has no rightful place on this earth,
besides destroying men and property, everything that is seen, it
destroys those unseen things, our senses, our sense of beauty,
happiness, comradeship amongst all men, anything that is worth
living for. Property is not essential. But happiness, a love of beauty,
friendship between all peoples and individuals, is life itself.

Secondly, you. I've put you second, I wonder if you feel that
strange. But this war affects everybody, I'd be very selfish if I put
you first in this thought, I'm trying to fathom out for myself. You
are just everything to me. The unforgivable way I write would make
another feel that you have been guilty of my loss in taking no notice
in the surrounding beauty, but you understand, I'm sure, that it is
only because I'm not constantly with you, that is the real factor.
You, Darling, have made me able to see, to feel and to understand,
all the beauty that is in the world, and life itself, without you that
understanding does not disappear, for you are with me constantly, in
my thoughts, but that understanding of life does seem to fade.

This war is keeping us apart, and therefore it is to blame in my
loss, and that loss is not only mine but of every person in the world
connected with the war.

I have never spoken to you of my feelings and thoughts about
this war, and I hope I will never speak of them again. Do you
remember a small boy saying he would be a conscientious objector
if war came? Things happened to change that small boy's views,
talk of brutality, human suffering, atrocities, but that did not have
any great effect on changing my mind for I realise that we all are
capable of doing these deeds of which we read so much nowadays.
It is the fact that a few people wish to take freedom from the
peoples of the earth that changed my views. News of atrocities only
breeds hate, and hate is contemptible in my eyes. I will never be
capable I hope of hating anyone whatever they have done.

Why should I then fight in the war which only brings disgust
into my thoughts?

It is so that I might live in happiness and peace all my days with you. You notice I put myself first, again it is a strange thing but I am trying hard to be honest with myself and I find that I, and consequently everybody, am terribly selfish, it is human nature, I'm afraid.

I am also fighting so that one day happiness will again rule the world, and with happiness that love of beauty, of life, contentment, fellowship among all men may return. You may again have noticed that I have not mentioned fighting for one's country, for the empire, that to me is just foolishness, for greatness in one nation will always breed hate and longing in another, and the whole of life will again be disrupted.

Mainly however, I'm fighting for the freedom of all men, and in that I am fighting just as much for the Germans as for the English people. With freedom and the destruction of hate this world will enter into a period which I hope will be much in advance of anything it has ever known.

When peace returns, and may it be soon, the world must make sure that the men and women of the future are educated in the right way, a love of beauty, not a love of war, and it is our own job to teach our children about all the loveliness of this world, to make them happy so that they can understand that love and happiness are the things really worth having.

Well, Darling, I seem to have been rambling on for some time, really I must stop. I don't know whether I have made any sense out of my ramblings, I only hope so.

Today's news is very small. I saw 'They Flew Alone' tonight, and I think I enjoyed it, I'm not quite sure.

'The Stars Look Down' although not a pleasant sort of book has held my interest and I'm reading solidly through it.

All my love, Darling, you mean so very much to me,
Always,
Laurie

Gwen has never been back to Shawbury, or Shrewsbury, since Laurie died: 'I couldn't, I want to remember it as it was.' She had been living in

this war which only brings disgust
into my thoughts?

It is so that I might live
in happiness and peace all my days
with you. You notice I put myself
first, again it is a strange thing,
but I am trying hard to be honest
with myself and I find that I, and
consequently everybody, am terribly selfish,
it is human nature.

I am also fighting so that
one day happiness will again rule the
world, and with happiness that love
of beauty, of life, contentment,
fellowship among all men may
return. You may again have noticed

a little village called Battlefield, and when her daughter Anne Marie was born, she went back there for eighteen months. 'It was hell going back to the same house. We were outside the village and completely isolated.'

Gwen brought up Anne Marie on her own, earning her living as a dress-maker and designer. She has never remarried.

IRENE GRUNDY
&
NEWTON ODDY

Irene Grundy was fifteen when she first saw Newton Oddy. He was working opposite her in the butcher's in Guildford High Street, and Irene was working in the Scotch Wool and Hosiery Stores. They waved to each other. She then started doing a bread round for Butler's Bakers, delivering by horse and cart. One day he pulled up in front of her as she was on her rounds, and asked her out. They both had bikes, liked going to the pictures, and, Irene being a tomboy, playing football.

When Newton (who Irene called 'Curly') was called up in December 1943, at the age of seventeen and a half, he asked Irene if she would be his girlfriend while he was in the forces. Irene agreed, and Curly went to report to the RAF in St John's Wood for training. 'Everyone liked him,' Irene says. 'My mum, my dad – he used to send them parcels, razor blades for my dad, and everybody on the bread round would ask me how he was getting on.' From St John's Wood Curly was sent to Bridlington for his initial training, and then to Bridgnorth. They wrote to each other, and Curly came home on leave for a week in February 1944, and for twenty-one days in May. 'We told each other everything in our letters. I'd sit up in bed and write to him about whatever was going on, it was like talking to him. In those days you got to know someone first as a person, rather than the *Fatal Attraction* it is now. It was a different world, very innocent. I didn't like him cuddling me in his uniform, the jacket was so rough, so he teased me that he'd strip off. It was that February leave in 1944 when he asked me to get engaged. We decided to marry after the war. He was studying very hard after that, doing his basic training as a navigator, and doing wireless training.'

Curly did not have a lot of time to write letters, but made it quite clear to Irene how important her writing to him was:

One thing about being away from you, I really can appreciate a letter. I'm so glad darling that you do write to me so often. You know that I'll always write to you whenever I can.

I often wonder what it would be like being separated from you, and loving you as I do, not to be able to exchange letters. It's the only link between us and I think it would be terrible if there were no such things as letters, don't you?

In August 1944 Curly set off for Nassau with Coastal Command. Irene began collecting for their bottom drawer. She bought a beautiful veil with embroidered scrolls all around it for herself, and headdresses for the bridesmaids, bedding, towels, teacloths, and started looking for material to make her wedding dress. When Curly came home on leave she always took everything out for him to see. By then they were officially engaged, and Irene had a locket that he had given her with a picture of himself in it on the left-hand side. They had planned everything together, it was going to be a white wedding.

'We never mentioned the possibility of his not coming back till his last leave, up till then most of what he'd been doing was training. Then he'd gone to Aldegrove in Northern Ireland. They'd gone on sorties from there over the Atlantic, looking for submarines. He had had a near-miss. He asked me to mend his flying suit. It looked as though it had been ripped by a knife. I asked him how he'd done it. He was a tail gunner, and a piece of shrapnel had gone right up the side of his leg and landed in the seat behind him. Curly said he'd been really frightened. I was scared stiff. It was the only time I ever heard him say that. We were both scared. It was the blind leading the blind. We both got upset, we both cried. I remember saying "You're definitely coming back," and we didn't refer to it again.

'We got very close on that December leave, it was becoming very difficult for him to behave himself. It wasn't looked on as very nice to make love before you married then, if you went to the altar in a white dress, you had to have earned the privilege.'

Irene came to stay with Curly on his leave in March, and he knocked on the door of the little end room she was in. He asked to be allowed to get into bed with her. They did not make love. 'He would never have taken advantage of me. He was always gentle. We lay there together and he just held me. It was the first time I had seen a man naked. It was quite a shock. When we woke up in the morning he went back to his room. We'd hoped to get married that May, but as things weren't ready, had postponed it till the August. It was all systems go for then.'

On 11 April 1945 Curly wrote to Irene openly agonizing about the dilemma they faced and shared. As two people in love, and able to communicate honestly and straightforwardly through their letters, he at once yearned for Irene but could not bear to think he had gone too far, overstepped the mark, and wrote of his overwhelming love and respect for her:

> 1851916 SGT ODDY E.N.
> ETC.!
> April 11, 1945

My Own,

At last I've had some mail from you. Actually I've had today eleven letters from you darling.

First I'd better apologise for my last letter. I thought, maybe, you'd put the wrong address on my letters but you hadn't. I'm sorry I wrote as I did dearest, but I was worried. Now I feel very happy. I never doubted you or anything silly like that when I didn't hear from you. And today I got eleven letters telling me how much you love and want me. No more than I love and want you though darling.

The letter I was most looking forward to getting, was the one in answer to the one I wrote about me 'easing up' a bit when I'm with you.

I'm glad you feel about it as you do darling. I feel the same as you. I could write and tell you now that I've no intentions of holding you close again. When I got with you again I'd lose some of my control and want to be close to you again. I don't want to hold you at arms length dearest, *I love you*, so, I want to hold you close to me and feel your lovely body against mine. I'll be honest with you darling. I want to do more than hold you close as I did on my last leave. I want a husbands "rights" darling. As we are not married though I shall have to wait a bit longer. I hope I don't sound a rake to you, but I'm just trying to tell you how I feel about you. It's just that I'm in love with you darling and now that I know you as I do, and am no longer shy with you, I'm afraid I want everything I can get out of our being together.

I hope I don't sound crude to you darling in my writing, it's just that it's such a job to put down on paper what I want to say. I know you will understand though, you always do. I know, too, that you must feel the same.

Now you know how I feel and I know how you feel. Do you think it will be wise for us to go on holiday together? I'd try and control myself darling and you know that if you said 'no' to anything, I wouldn't do it. I don't want you to have to put me in my place dearest because that would upset you and I don't want to do that.

Well dearest I hope I haven't offended you in anything I have said. If I have, please forgive me. I love you darling and am missing you more than I can say. I've got no girlfriend here (and don't want one unless it is you) to unburden my thoughts to. So you see darling anything I think of, especially that which worries me, as our being together does, I'm going to unburden myself on you.

There's nothing to tell you about of this dump I'm in dear so, I don't quite know what else to write about. I feel I want to tell you so much but when I get down to writing I can't think of much to tell you. All I really want is a letter from you saying you love me, then I can sit down and write to you and say – I LOVE YOU TOO.

I do wish we could get married soon darling then I shouldn't have to write as I have done tonight. As we are now though, I feel sort of unsettled so the sooner we are married and can be together always, the better I shall feel. I hope what I'm going to say now won't upset you. You said 'If I hadn't been brought up so well' etc. you would have let yourself in for the pudding club long ago. Of all the crude sayings darling, I think that's the worst. I'm really surprised that you should use it. I know you're no angel as you put it but please darling don't say anything like that again. I think the world of you darling and I think (or should I say know) that when you are carrying *our* child you wouldn't like to be referred to in that way.

Enough of that dearest, I'm afraid I shall have to close all together soon. I shall have to get some sleep in. It's going to be a job to change my habits on leave. I sleep all day now and "go out" at night so I shall be wide awake when you're thinking about bed.

You really did tempt me in one letter when you said you were sitting in front of the fire in your pyjamas and everyone was out. Why don't people go out when I'm home? (I've never seen you in pyjamas come to that). I remember you in a night dress. Best of all though I remember you on our last night together in a green slip. It was a wonder I didn't "slip". I often wonder how the devil I kept control of myself. I don't think I'd try very hard to control myself if I see you like that on my next leave darling! That's being honest again isn't it?

That's how I feel about you darling so I thought I'd tell you. Please dearest, in your next letter tell me how you feel about things when we are together. Don't be afraid to tell me, I shall understand and I want to know. You see darling I still wonder if maybe I have gone too far. Only you can tell me whether I have or not and if you want me to ease up.

What I want to know most of all though is if you think we ought to go on this holiday together. I want to but, what of the temptations?

I'll close now my love. I'm longing to get an answer to this queer (?) letter.

My love as always my love. I'm yours for *always*.
God Bless you,
Yours Newton

PS RSVP is French for answer as soon as possible. RSVP!!!

On 25 April Irene received official notification that Curly was 'missing, presumed dead'. 'Up till then I used to wait for every letter to drop on the mat to tell me he was all right. Once he'd gone, his last letters still arrived, until one day there was nothing. That nothing was terrible. I didn't believe he'd died till then. It was worse almost than when I was told he'd been killed.'

Curly's last letter was written three days before his death:

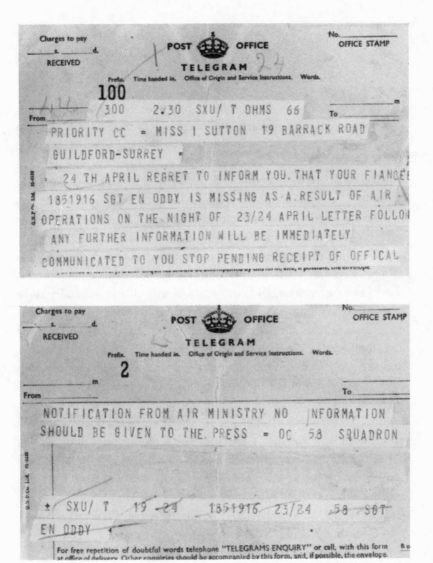

Charges to pay s. d. RECEIVED

No. OFFICE STAMP

POST ✠ OFFICE
TELEGRAM

Prefix. Time handed in. Office of Origin and Service Instructions. Words.

100

/300   2.30   SXU/ T OHMS 66

From ___   To ___   m

PRIORITY CC = MISS I SUTTON 19 BARRACK ROAD
GUILDFORD-SURREY =
24 TH APRIL REGRET TO INFORM YOU. THAT YOUR FIANCEE
1851916 SGT EN ODDY IS MISSING AS A RESULT OF AIR
OPERATIONS ON THE NIGHT OF 23/24 APRIL LETTER FOLLOW
ANY FURTHER INFORMATION WILL BE IMMEDIATELY
COMMUNICATED TO YOU STOP PENDING RECEIPT OF OFFICAL

Charges to pay s. d. RECEIVED

No. OFFICE STAMP

POST ✠ OFFICE
TELEGRAM

Prefix. Time handed in. Office of Origin and Service Instructions. Words.

2

m
From ___   To ___

NOTIFICATION FROM AIR MINISTRY NO INFORMATION
SHOULD BE GIVEN TO THE PRESS = OC 58 SQUADRON

± SXU/ T 19 -24   1851916 23/24 58 SGT
EN ODDY +

For free repetition of doubtful words telephone "TELEGRAMS ENQUIRY" or call, with this form
at office of delivery. Other enquiries should be accompanied by this form, and, if possible, the envelope.

RAF Box 200
GLASGOW

April 22nd, 1945

Irene dearest,

I'm sorry I haven't written for a couple of days but I've been enjoying myself somewhere in England.

It was lovely to see trees and green grass again. Where we were there were daffodils and primroses growing wild and birds too. Not seagulls! The roads were dusty too, it hadn't rained for days. It was so hot too that the tar stuck to our boots and the wheels of our aircraft (which hasn't got a name).

You might wonder why I am writing about these everyday things. You see, darling, this place is barren. No trees, rain and wind nearly every day, and thousands of seagulls. Incidentally these seagulls always seem to pick on me for their dive bombing attacks.

If your papers for Saturday 21st of April haven't been burnt or lost, look up the bit with the gen. about Halifaxes bombing a ship in the Skaggerack and you'll know why I've been in England two days. If you can find the bit cut it out and post it here.

I've had your letter answering my eleven page effort darling. It's nice to know you feel the same about things as I do. That last night we spent together I felt just the same as you. You were so close to me and I was so much in Love with you that I almost said 'To hell with principles' too. It's a good job we can't read one another's thoughts isn't it darling?

One thing after your letter, no matter what we do in future, I won't worry any more. Your letter sure put my mind at rest. Thank you darling. It's funny darling I've worried about lots of things, especially when I was overseas. If only I'd known you then as I know you now. All I need have done was to have told you and your next letter would have put me right. You're a genius darling! I don't know what I'd do without you now. I guess I'd just be lost.

Lis and dad are very good to me but only you can answer some things. I'll make sure that I never upset you by keeping my thoughts from you again. Don't you keep anything from me either! Thanks for the gen on how your letters get posted. I hope I didn't sound as if I was worrying about it. Honestly darling, I wasn't. As usual, I was just inquisitive! Now I know why you don't want to go to dances when I'm home. It would be a dead loss for us to go dancing. I'd want to dance with you all the time and that wouldn't be fair! I've got you for myself and I'm keeping it that way. It'll always be that way dearest, you're mine and I'm yours for *always*.

People say always is a long time. But, if it was possible I could be with you longer than that and not get tired of you. I'll never tire of you my precious, *I love* you.

Again I'm like you. I want us to be married officially so that our combined love as you put it, can get together and we can have what you want. (You'd better make it a girl though!) One that I can watch grow up to be as lovely and good as you.

I close now dearest (it's tea time!). God Bless you and all at '19'.

All my love darling,
Yours Newton
xxxxxxxxxxx

Mrs. E N Grundy looks O.K. but I prefer:-
Mrs. *Irene* Grundy
Love the husband of the above xxxxxxxxxxxxxxxxx

After Curly's death, Irene joined the WAAF. 'I never mentioned what had happened, not even to my best friend Gay. It was my secret. I could talk about anything else, but not that. I didn't look at the letters then, I couldn't cope with it. Nobody talked about it at home, even the people on the bread round, they all tiptoed around it. I'd gone from having something big in my life to nothing, I was lost. The letters and photographs are all there is left of him. I don't want him – or all of them in that situation – to be forgotten. We were already married in terms of if anything bothered one of us we'd tell the other. His father gave me all my letters to him back, but I tossed them on the fire. They were not mine, they were his. They were more painful to me than his letters.'

Irene feels that Curly had changed a lot from the early days of their relationship to later in the war when he started doing operational things.

He became a different person, more serious, and his letters changed, he had grown up.

Looking back, aware that she had, in one sense, been keeping Curly at arm's length, Irene regrets that they never made love: 'He was getting on for twenty, in the prime of his life. He died without knowing, he had never been with a woman. I regret it now, that was what he was wanting to do. The holiday he mentions in his letter I'd suggested so we could be on our own. It was very important to men in his position then, not to die without knowing.'

Irene finally married when she was thirty-nine. She met her husband Eric when he came to run his taxi business from an office at the end of her restaurant. They live in Buckinghamshire.

JOAN HATFIELD
&
GEORGE HULL

'My mother was alone when the telegram came. She was never the same again, he was her boy.'

When Joan Hatfield's brother John died she was twenty, he was twenty-three. 'It was the first death we'd experienced, we were all broken-hearted. He was training in Winnipeg and engaged to a Canadian girl, Grace, so when he was at home on leave in London he took me out. We were very close. I met all his friends, and he taught me how to dance. I'm sure my brother knew he was going to die. He was stationed at Bitteswell near Rugby with the RAF. On his last leave he was reluctant to go back, he just sat at home playing his music. He knew he wasn't coming back.'

Joan had been called up into the Navy, and was stationed in Lancashire when the news came through of John's death: 'I'd only just been called up. Divisions [the twice-daily roll call] were at 5p.m., and I had to go and see a Wren officer, a cow, who had just turned to me and said: "Of course you know your brother was killed last night. Your father wants you to go home. I'll give you a railway warrant. Where do you live?" I couldn't remember for the life of me where I lived. I finally got to Manchester, where I boarded a train full of troops, and headed back home. It was terrible when I got there. His aircraft had exploded on landing and caught fire. He'd crashed in Stratford-on-Avon, thick fog had obscured everything, he was trying to land at Wellesbourne, and he'd overshot the runway and crashed. I went with my father to Watford station where we were met by the coffin and Union Jack, I don't know how we got through it, but we brought him home. I remember the dog sitting with him for what seemed like days. It was all a bit unreal then. His great friends George and Philip then insisted on coming with me all the way back to the gates of the camp in Lancashire. I knew about John's friend George Hull, but that was the first time I met him, at my brother's funeral.'

John had written his last letter home to the family on 24 June 1943. On the night of 2 July he died.

After their meeting, Joan and George started to correspond. To begin with, George was anxious to keep in touch with the family, but although meeting was difficult, with their leaves either not coinciding or being changed, the friendship became much more. George wrote fifty-one letters to Joan altogether, and as they wrote, their trust in each other grew, and the relationship became more of a romance.

George was an only child who had been brought up in Stepney, in

East London. He joined the RAF some time after the outbreak of war, and trained as a navigator. He loved the comradeship and the flying, but felt disaffection with the RAF, lacked confidence in those in command, and questioned his role in the war. He had an acute sense of his own mortality, and experienced bouts of depression, which resulted from close friends being killed all around him: 'I hate the RAF, this camp in particular, I hate the job we do, not for myself but for those who are lost in the gamble but I do like to fly it fascinates me', he wrote to Joan in November 1943.

On 1 February 1944 George wrote to Joan with his emotions clearly raised by a trip home, and an awareness of the danger of their strong feelings for one another in such an uncertain and dangerous climate. He struggled with his feelings of certainty of Joan's importance to him and his understanding that the closer their feelings brought them, the more difficult would be a final parting, if it were to come.

Coningsby
Tuesday, Midnight

My Dear Joan,

The hour is late, and I've just returned from leave this very minute, and clutched your letter with a great deal of delight. However, even though the bed is yet unmade, the news from the boys on the squadron is not so good, and my spirits otherwise low, I feel that I must write to you at once – you have that effect on me.

You will receive my letter written during leave before this one, so I will not waste time with a repeat of it all, sufficient to say that it passed in a flash and a dazzle, and without the satisfaction of having seen you for only a little while.

I am distressed and annoyed dear to hear that the place is no better than I imagined – I've flown often over Arran, Kintyre, Islay and Jura, and appreciated its singular beauty even from the air, but for you to be posted there for God knows how long makes me wild.

It does seem that Fate takes a hand in all our plans, but my reaction is to fight her for the little pleasures we ask. My only explanation is a bitter one: I could get a great deal fonder of you if I saw you more often – I remember the weekend at Manchester all too vividly – and perhaps it would not be fair. Not fair to me because it disturbs my peace of mind, unfair to you because what little interest you may have in me might be one day a grief to you equal almost to that which you have lately suffered. I don't want to labour the question of danger in this job like a little tin hero – braver men have died for better things – but I do want you to know that what I said at Skellingthorpe about the girl who inspires me, still holds. It may sound silly and insincere, perhaps, it is nevertheless true, witness my letter writing now, at such an ungodly hour!

As I read through the last few lines, I am inclined to laugh at 'Because it disturbs my peace of mind'. It sounds so smug – what I really mean is that when I think of you, I want to hold on to life with both hands and get out of the War somehow to live in certainty – a dangerous idea when it is for people like you that I will fight this to the end.

Being human however, I shall fight fate and those sacrificial ideas; already the Skipper and I have discussed the possibilities of a trip in your region when the days get longer and opportunity knocks. He's all for it! It's a remote, wild scheme but then so are we. Possibly our leaves can be 'engineered', we get leave every six weeks now, you know.

Meanwhile, I will write as often as I can, that at least gives me great satisfaction.

Latest news from your dad, from the hospital, that your Mum is still going along well, she is very cheerful indeed.

Cheerio then pet,

Yours always,
George

By then Joan was a telephonist at a little wireless station on the Mull of Kintyre, listening out every night for any ships in trouble. If a ship was in trouble, they were allowed to use their wireless, but not identify themselves, and if Joan got a coded signal, she shot it up to the watch as fast as she could for decoding.

George's letter refers to a weekend the two of them had snatched, that set a seal on their relationship, where they met at the Midland Hotel in Manchester, and went to Chester. 'The relationship didn't have a chance to take off. We got to know each other through our letters, and to know each other very well. He was a very bright chap, I was the naïvest Wren imaginable. I felt he was light years ahead, and admired him tremendously. He got on very well with my parents. I think we'd probably have married if he'd lived. England would have been a different place if all these good men had lived.'

On 26 February 1944 George wrote to Joan full of fierce disillusion, coupled with a clear understanding of the necessities of war and of their being totally at odds with what he held dear and true:

Well they have not killed us yet, although in saner moments when I think back to these lively little affairs I wonder why. It made me burn with rage on Thursday night as we were going over Schweinfurt to see the raid in London going on, I thought of your father and mine underneath it all, and I would not have turned back if we had caught fire. It rather added to my belief in the ultimate futility of all this slaughter though. As you mentioned in your last letter, John would have hated it all, my feelings are similar but I never lose sight of the fact that if our feelings rule our judgment, we might suffer terrible consequences.

. . . Of course I hate the job, but Idealism is not enough, as I said before, I am fighting for the people I love, and the boys who have already paid the full price. To give in to matters on ideological grounds is to let them all down . . . Please forgive this letter, its contents and the writing. I have a 'post-ops' headache, feel worked out completely, and as usual fed-up to the back teeth.

I will write tomorrow given the chance.

Cheerio dear, your feelings are my consolation –

Yours always,
George

Three weeks later he was dead. His poignant letter convinced Joan that George knew he wouldn't return. He unloaded a lot of his fears, worries and gloom in his letters, and there is also a sense of how desperately worn out he was, going out on operations every other night.

It was while Joan was on leave with her family in Watford that the telegram came to say George was missing. He had gone out on the night of 18 March 1944 in a Lancaster bomber, and was lost on a raid to Germany.

'When I think back, I was so stupid. I should have dropped everything, and just gone to the airfield where he was stationed. Risked the wrath of the authorities, and comforted him, spent some time with him. I lost practically every man I knew in the war, they all died, boyfriends, schoolfriends, they all went. At the end of the war, there was nobody living I knew, I had no old friends left. I'm sure that's why there were so many disastrous marriages after the war. We'd all changed so much by the end of it.

'George had spent so much time at our house that he'd put our family down as one of those to be informed if he died. His aircraft had come down, so we assumed that if he wasn't dead, he'd either tried to get out via lifelines, or we'd eventually hear if he'd been captured. Three or four months later the aircraft was found, after the period of not knowing. I think it was found unmarked and against a tree. There was a wedding ring found in his top pocket. My father had told me that the weekend before he'd gone missing, George had telephoned him to ask him if he could marry me. I remember writing to him at one stage, and saying take someone else out. I knew the war was going to keep us apart, and I wanted him to have a girlfriend on the base, to live a bit. I had a boyfriend in Mull. The words mean something different now, but I had someone to take me out dancing. I didn't want George to write to me every night rather than going out. I felt awful after I'd written it, I regretted it, and I felt he didn't want me to have said it.'

When the body had been recovered, it was taken to Drumbach War Cemetery near Munich where George was buried with the rest of his crew.

Looking back, Joan finds it extraordinary how a relationship survived on so few meetings. 'It was hope, optimism that did it.' But when he went missing it seemed final. 'During the missing period we didn't think we'd ever see him again. We were all prepared for a final letter. It wasn't such a deep wound as when my brother died. When George died I accepted it as inevitable, I was almost prepared for it. George is gone. They were all gone, they were all dying. I kept in touch with his father who was a real source of strength to me. I began to resent being ordered around, the lack of freedom, you couldn't do anything, your life was taken away from you.'

On 29 July 1944, Joan wrote home to her parents illustrating bitterly the everyday nature of death and the awfulness of being left behind:

Words cannot express how I hate this war, the parting from people, the loneliness that is always with you, the losing of people you love and who love you. Without even saying goodbye. Sometimes I feel so sad that I almost wish I were dead too. Seems a silly thing to say but death is so apparent here all the time.

A month later, on 26 August, Joan reiterated her sense of loss:

Why should any of these boys die, sometimes it seems to me that they are the lucky ones and that we who are left behind are the ones who are unhappy and lonely. Practically all my friends have gone now . . .

Joan's relationship with George left an indelible mark: 'It still influences me today. I often think of him. A few years ago I went through a very bad patch. One awful night I went to sleep and saw him, and he took my left hand and I felt quite comforted when I woke up, and stronger. He certainly influenced me – I often think if there's a problem, what would George have done? I was still getting over John's death when George wrote and said he'd meet me anywhere in the world. I didn't realize how deep his feelings for me were till then. Letters were the one stable thing. They were so poignant, they had an extraordinary effect. Without them you were just adrift in a strange world. And George was the rock in a shifting world. He was writing his last letter to me over a period of months. The things he said to me in his letters over a long period were a last letter. What he'd done, what he was doing it for, what had made him stay, what his hopes were, how he wanted us to get on, about his love of music, his love of England. His letters gave me an identity in a world in which I was totally and unexpectedly relying on myself, and where otherwise I had no identity outside my war job.'

Joan has since married, and lives in Devon. She is still planning to visit George's grave near Munich one day.

JUNE BENNETT
&
JAMES BELL

F/O James (Hamish) Bell DFM first met June Mary Bennett in September 1941 at the RAF wedding of a close friend. He was the best man, she was the bridesmaid. June was sixteen, James was twenty-one. Eventually, James plucked up the courage to write to June on 6 January 1942.

It's almost 3½ months since we met at Viv and Joyce's wedding. As I've kept in touch with them, I thought the least I could do was to drop you a few lines & see how the world's abusing you . . .

. . . I shall never forget their wedding. It was such a happy event and I met such fine people there, especially the 'younger ones' no names, no pack drill . . . Don't be afraid to write a few lines . . .

About a month later,

I don't see why you should be nervous of 'us men'. After all we are human, or are we? But I must admit I, too, do not feel altogether at home when in the company of the 'fair sex' but as you say, it's probably due to shyness and Scottish reserve.

According to June, the couple 'just clicked' when they met and their relationship developed from there, albeit very slowly. She had been at boarding school since the age of ten and was used to being self-contained. James was 'a true Scotsman brought up to be a gentleman. He was reserved and shy, proud to be Scottish, loved the land and he spoke English better than us down south.' When they met, June was about to start training to be a nurse. James was an air gunner 'performing one of the most dangerous jobs there was. We always knew his chances of survival were slender. And that's why he was very sure and felt strongly that we had no right to marry while the war was on. I accepted this.'

As James was based in Leamington, June in Oswestry, his parents in Scotland, hers in London, even when leave coincided, it was complicated for them to meet. James wrote:

. . . nowadays, it's very seldom that a chap is so lucky as to find a friend as sensible as you are. It's very true what you say, the more one knows about another the closer their friendship . . . I'm looking forward to being in London and needless to say, I am also looking forward to seeing you . . .

They met a few days later, their first leave together, June remembers: 'We were very guarded on the emotional side, we held hands, we kissed but we didn't go to bed together, like today's people. I remember going to the park and eating cherries together and then spitting out the stones . . . that sort of thing.' James wrote on 20 April:

After I left you last night, I went into the tube and travelled round the inner circle about three times before I finally managed to branch off to Paddington . . . I sincerely hoped you enjoyed the weekend as much as I did. It is something I shall remember for a long long time . . . not because I was in London . . . but because I was with you. We must try and wangle another weekend, sometime soon . . .

James's work was becoming more stressful. He stopped going on ops and was now lecturing students for up to seven hours a day. There were many casualties while on training which upset him. Life at the training camp was so unpredictable that his leave dates were very loose. Each arrangement was a maybe or hoping for an uninterrupted weekend.

In May 1942, the war was going badly for the Allies. According to James 'the RAF's success is due to the fact that it is a new service to new ideas and has no tradition to tie it down . . . Our army and Navy are too old fashioned for modern warfare . . .'

But the pressure was on to achieve more. On 2 June he wrote,

You mean a great deal to me now, especially after our last weekend, of which every minute I thoroughly enjoyed . . . It does relieve one to tell their troubles to someone else. Specially if the other person is sympathetic.

June was understanding. 'If I showed my anxiety, what chance did he have?' And so she continued to write two or three letters to every one James sent. In mid-June he wrote

Thanks a million for both your letters. I've kept all your letters and I read over them from time to time when I am feeling 'blue'.

As the summer wore on, close friends of James were killed, and he was feeling very 'browned off'. Because he was stationed in England, his letters weren't censored and he was able to write of his concern about the punishing training course; too many were being killed or wounded and tension and stress exhausted him. 'He preferred to fight and be flying.' On 8 December, June received a letter just after a leave they had spent together. He was obviously going through a bad patch:

Officers Mess
Wellesbourne
Warwickshire

My Dearest June,

First of all I wish to thank your mother and father and you very very much indeed for the marvellous two days. I enjoyed every minute of my short stay. In fact during the past few days in sacred silence I have mentally lived through it again and again each time remembering something new, the merest detail, perhaps a gesture or a word, done or spoken deeply, truthfully and sincerely which I shall cherrish in my heart and remember for ever.

I will give you a brief summary of what has happened up to date from the time I left you goodbye at the bus stop.

The bus I mounted only went about 50 yrds along the road to the bus depot. I walked from there crossed the bridge turned right instead of left got lost and had to ask directions from at least 6 different people before I eventually got seated in the train with two minutes to spare. I arrived at Paddington got into the correct train and fell asleep. I was wakened at Leamington by an Army type who was travelling in the same compartment. On the platform I met the other chaps from Wellesbourne, couldn't get a taxi so finally made our way to an army hut where we dozed by a big fire until 6am. From there we walked about a mile to a small café in heavy rain to get a cup of tea. We caught a bus at seven and arrived in camp about 8, cold, wet and feeling a bit miserable. However after a good breakfast I felt much better and was in the air by nine.

While I was away, a squadron leader who has come up here to pick up a crew asked the Chief Instructor if he could have me for his gunner. The C.I. said he would let me go if I wanted to so now I am just waiting for the confirmation to come through from Group. How it stands at present is that in the very near future, with a bit of luck I shall officially become a pupil again.

Yes, I am sure a change will do me the world of good, and apart from that, as far as I can see, there is very little chance of promotion here. Of course, we are promised lots of things if we stay on but I've realised now that these promises never materialise, they are just part of a scheme to keep us from getting browned off. I am sure you will agree with me when I say that without the possibility of promotion one is inclined to get into a rut. Anyway, I shall be much happier on an operational station.

I do hope your Mum's interview is successful and that the Exchange fix her up with an interesting job. I also hope she is hearing regularly from your Dad and that he is in the best of health. It must certainly be a trying time for your Mum.

I must close down now as it is bed time. I will write again in a few days time.

Goodnight June
wishing you every success in your new post

All my fondest love and kisses
Jimmy

Their next leave was in February, but afterwards James wasn't able to write to June until 2 April: 'The memories of our last night together are very fresh in my mind.' He was apologetic about the long gap between

Posted missing last night
June 25.

Miss June N. Bennett.

Surbiton Hospital

Ewell Road.

Surbiton

letters but by now he was on tours over Germany and North Africa. On 25 June, he wrote:

Now about this leave question. I am due for some next month but there is no definite date laid down as yet. However, I shall do my very best so that some part of my leave will coincide with yours and we can spend a weekend together.

This was the last letter he wrote. His aircraft was blown up. June remembers: 'I was living at the hospital at the time. When my last letter was returned "missing", I couldn't believe it. For six months I was hoping to hear he was a POW. On the night of his death, four other planes didn't come back. No bodies were found. He has no grave. I lived for his letters. I would sit down and write long letters to him – I had more time than he. We didn't talk about things that would make him anxious. He was more anxious about me, living in the Blitz in London, than about himself.'

About a year and a half after James's death, June went to Argyllshire to meet his family. She became friendly and ultimately very close to them and still sees them today. June never married. James was her first love: 'After his death, I didn't feel I wanted to marry, to look after one man – that's not my scene. I decided to devote my life to others. I studied, had a career and now look after elderly people.'

June keeps James's letters by her bedside and, now and again, she rereads them.

PART V

Separation & Return

ALBERT &
GLADYS READ

C/O P.O. Box 164
London L.C.I.
Sept., 17th, 1945

My Darling Gladys,

Thousands of years ago, someone for the first time started to do something. What we now know as to write. Of course it was very likely signs vastly different from our alphabet. I wonder if it ever occurred to that person how great would be his best gift to man in centuries to follow.

Take we two for example, without correspondence would we have ever met? Would the love we now feel towards each other, have burnt as fiercely as it does now? Would we as two independent persons ever have known how fiercely love could burn? If we had partnered our lives off with two other people. You and I know the answer to all these questions, the answer we know is no.

It was fate that brought us together darling, yes, the same ironic fate that dominates people's lives, bringing both happiness and sorrow in their turn. To us it has given a share of both in the last six years. First happiness in our meeting then a never to be forgotten sorrow. Now we will be happy again, I with you, and you with my undying devotion.

We shall have our ups and downs during our lives, but with you darling, I feel in my heart that I could bear almost anything, so long as we are together. I love you darling more than anything in this world and nothing will make me do otherwise. I have never really spoken these words to you, not even during those Oh so short times we were together dear. Please forgive me my sweet, we were both young then. I never have doubted your love for me. Even if I had of done so you have proved your sincerity by so patiently and faithfully waiting for me.

When I recall that incident on the second night of my leave in August 1940, I feel ashamed of myself, and know that I acted like a silly school boy. If this sounds melodramatic, I ask forgiveness as I have often pondered over it, and know now that I have let golden moments slip through my fingers.

I can only wait patiently now, for my return home. Then I shall show you with the words and actions of a man, that I really and truly love you and care for you darling. The future holds many surprises for us both, but you and I will face them together, and if needs be our love will make our sorrowful moments happy and our happy ones, bliss.

I can hardly wait for the day when I shall be with you and everyone again.

I shall always do my best to be to you my darling, what I know you would want me to be. Your ever loving and devoted sweetheart.

Love to you darling and all at home.

I am at all times your ever loving and devoted,
Albert xxxxxxxxxxxxxxx
'DEEP PURPLE'

Albert and Gladys Read met by letter. Theirs was a wartime romance conducted mostly by pen. They had only met briefly over a ten-day period before they were separated for five years and one month. When war was declared, Bert, aged seventeen, and already in the Territorial Army, was called up. His elder brother had joined two years before him. His brother, a fully trained radio operator, was sent to Crewkerne in Somerset, while Bert, still a green signalman 'rookie', stayed in Chiswick. Bert suffered from paralysing shyness, and instead of going out with the lads wrote letters in his spare time. One of the letters he wrote was to his elder brother's girlfriend. By return he had a letter back, thanking him for the photograph he had sent, and asking him whether he minded a young cousin of hers from Bridgwater, who was keen to write to someone in the forces, getting in touch. Her name was Gladys Marion Watkins. A letter arrived from her in the same post.

'We became pen-friends, and after a few letters, something seemed to "click" between us. I was then eighteen, she sixteen.' Bert felt that their letters helped them to get to know each other in a way that they never would have done with an ordinary courtship: 'I got to know her by letter. I was able to tell her everything, including the things about me I thought a girl wouldn't like, my shyness, my glasses. Your nature comes out in your writing. We both liked cycling and music. You get to know more

c/o P.O. Box 164
London E.C.1
Sept, 17th 1945.

My darling Gladys,

Thousands of years ago, someone for the first time, started to do something, that we now know as 'to write.' Of course it was very likely, signs vastly different from our alphabet. I wonder if it ever occurred to that person how great would be his gift to man in centuries to follow? Take we two for example, without 'correspondence' would we have ever met, would the love we now feel towards each other, burnt so fiercely as it does now, would it as two independent persons we have known how freshly love could grow if we had fashioned our lives off with two other people. You and I know the answer to all these questions, the answer we know is no.

It was fate that brought us together darling, yes, the same ironic fate that dominates people's lives,

bringing both happiness & sorrow in their train. To us it has given a share of both in the last six years. First happiness in our meeting, then a sorrow to be forgotten sorrow. Now we will be happy again, I with you, and you with my undying devotion.

We shall have our ups and downs during our lives, but with you darling I feel in my heart that I could bear almost anything, as long as we were together. I love you darling more than anything in this world and nothing will make me do otherwise. I have never really spoken these words to you, not even during those all so short time we were together dear. Please believe me my sweet, you were both young then. I never have doubted your love for me. Even if I had of done so you have proved your sincerity by patiently and faithfully waiting for me.

When I recall the incident that on the second night of leave in August 1940, I feel ashamed of myself and know that I agg—

about a person through letters than when you meet them and they're on their best behaviour. It was the inner person I got to know.'

At last came an opportunity to meet. Bert was due a week's leave from where he'd been moved in Surrey, and Gladys's mother told her to invite him down to Somerset rather than London because of the night bombing. When the day arrived, Bert was so nervous, that he didn't get to Paddington until 5.00 p.m., and the 5.00 p.m. train had gone. In a complete panic he sent a telegram, something he had never done before, and waited for the next train at 6.00 p.m. It was due in at Bridgwater at 10.15 p.m., 'but because it had to pass through towns and cities at a much reduced speed so that sparks wouldn't be seen by possible bombers, it was well after 11.15 p.m. when it slowly pulled into the dimly lit country station. On looking out of the window I had spotted Gladys still waiting for me. On seeing her, I was overcome with shyness, so that when I stepped down from the train, some fifty yards from her, I didn't look her way, instead I went up to a large red chocolate machine, fumbling in my pocket for a penny. Then a small form appeared by my side. "Are you Mr Read?" At my mumbled "Yes" came the response, "I'm Gladys." By this time in our correspondence we had got to the stage of signing off "Your loving sweetheart", so that when we had written of the forthcoming trip, we had discussed whether we would kiss or shake hands. Such was my shyness when we did meet, I thrust my hand out, and we shook hands – an eighteen-year-old soldier and a sixteen-year-old slip of a girl.'

They kissed twice during their seven days together, the first time on their second night. As they told me about it Bert reminded Gladys of a long letter he wrote to her aboard SS *Chitral* on his return home from POW camp in October 1945: 'Do you also remember the night you showed me the back entrance to Mr and Mrs Norman's house, and how I was too shy to kiss you goodnight? When I was walking towards the house I felt as if I could kick myself but then it happened. You called me back, and I almost ran back. Then you kissed me and hurried home. That night I could hardly sleep and it wasn't with insomnia either. All I could do was to lie there hugging the pillow; and think of our first kiss. The kiss that was to bind our two lives together.'

They met again briefly later that year when Bert was on leave, before he went overseas, and Gladys joined the National Fire Service. They wrote constantly, although it often took up to three months for letters to arrive to and from the Far East. Then the war in the Far East broke out, and on Bert's twentieth birthday, 15 February 1942, he became a Japanese prisoner-of-war in Singapore. It was eighteen months before any of his family or loved ones at home knew that he was still alive. He wrote the usual POW cards, but mostly they didn't get through. His time in the camp was harrowing: thirteen stone when he was first taken prisoner, Bert weighed six stone when he was liberated.

'The only thing that occupied my mind was where I'd get food from. You came to accept death, to become mercenary about it. When someone died, it was a question of who's going to have his blanket.'

But there were two certainties in his mind from which he never wavered. 'I never thought about not coming home, and I never thought Gladys wouldn't be waiting for me.'

Bert is still unable to talk about his years in prisoner-of-war camp, he finds it too traumatic, but on 15 August 1945 he was freed, and moved down from the jungle in Siam to Bangkok, where he was flown to Rangoon. It was from there that a free cable was sent home to say he was safe. He immediately wrote to the girl he hadn't seen for five years.

> Sept. 14th, 1945
> C/O P.O. Box 164
> London L.C.I.

Darling Gladys,

Words to express my feelings at being able to once more write to you, have yet to be composed. You must excuse my first few attempts at letter writing after three and a half years, writing one post-card on an average of seven month periods has somewhat dulled my mind.

The years I have spent as a P.O.W. were dark years, lightened only by mail from England. The 'Nips' didn't bother hardly at all with mail, and so the distribution of letters was very haphazard. I received approx. twelve of your letters darling, a very small percentage of what I know you must have written. The last letter that I received was dated 5/6/43 in which several very interesting things are mentioned.

You tell me you have altered a lot since I last saw you dear, you must send me a photo of yourself so that I will be able to recognise you, not that I think that I won't be able to, but it is such a long time since I have been able to look at someone beautiful. I have been able to keep two photographs of you darling, one which was taken at Weston – during that first heavenly seven days I spent with you in August 1940, memories of which often helped me while away some of the darkest moments as a P.O.W. I wonder if you still recall that second night I was with you in the front room, and the incident which happened, helped me to get over my shyness enough to make the rest of my holiday heaven? I'm sure you do. And the evening we went for a walk and got lost. Also the trip to the cinema. All these and lots more memories of our golden hours together dearest have made me love you more and more, and have also made me long for the day when I shall hold you close to me again.

I always knew that Sylvia was as clever as her sister. I hope, she has enjoyed her learning at the County School for girls. When I last saw Sylvia she was if I remember correctly seven years old, she will have grown a lot since then, but ask her if she still remembers the game she got me to play with her when I was there in 1940. It was a piece of cardboard with rows of holes stamped in it on which you made designs and patterns with coloured clay marbles. If Sylvia remembers this, she will also remember putting a marble into my tunic pocket. Tell her I still have it.

I am looking forward to seeing Beryl's baby son. But most of all I am looking forward to seeing you again darling. Now that the war is over we can think more seriously of life. When I read the news in your letter, I was as pleased as a dog with two tails.

I must tell you dearest that in their letters Mum and Rita have told me that they think the world of you. That goes for me too. My love for you is limitless, there are no boundaries to my desire to be with you always. My Darling, I shall write often to you and one day, I have a question to ask you.

Cheerio for now dearest. You are ever in my thoughts, and I shall always be your devoted sweetheart,

Albert xxxxxxxxxxxx

The moment Gladys received Bert's cable, she wrote:

22 Angel Crescent
Bridgwater
Somerset
ENGLAND

19-9-45

My Darling Albert,

To me it is as though I am writing this letter in a dream, that I am afraid to wake up and find – my darling how you must feel I just cannot think, I am so terribly happy to know my dear that you are safe and coming back, we are waiting for you dear. I am waiting with outstretched arms to welcome you home and care for you.

I wonder dear if you will still think of me as you did so long ago. I have grown up dear, and folks say I have changed, for the better, all that is worrying me dear is that you will still see me as you did when you left me as someone who loves you and wants you very much.

I do hope you are well, that you have every comfort my dear, millions of thoughts must be passing through your mind at this time. Thoughts of being home after all you have suffered, thoughts of being with those you love, and those who love you.

Your Mum and I have been writing together and since you went away, she has been marvellous to me, always keeping me informed of news from you, and sending me your cards to read, she has been good to me darling.

I expect you wonder what I have been doing all this time – well my sweetheart I have been a telephonist in the Fire Service for 3 years, I may be out soon now but dear I have still got 14 days leave saved up for when you come home, and whatever you wish to do then dear, will be all right with me. I mean if you want to come here dear or me come to London, you have only got to say. Remember Sylvia dear, she is still at school, and still has the handkerchief you sent her from Malaya. Peter is working in a Garage. Mum and Dad are still all right, on the 1st of October we are moving houses darling and are going to live in High Street, in a licensed house the address will be

'Old Oak Inn'
20 High Street,
Bridgwater

My brother Len is in India in the army, he is married now. Do you remember Beryl my cousin? She is married and has got two babies.

I remember so well dear all the golden hours I spent with you. When we are together again we must make up for all the time we have lost, I have kept every one of your letters darling and telegrams and photos.

I hope you like the photo I am sending you of myself, I have always kept your photograph at my bedside and have kissed it every night. I am longing for a letter from you, but most of all I am waiting and longing to see you again, I do hope this letter has made you happy and everything I have said in it was what you wanted to hear, of all the songs I have heard never has one beaten 'Deep Purple' it means everything to you and I darling. Please dear, do whatever you want to do when you get home, but remember me and I will do whatever you want of me.

It has been so long for me, all so very terrible for you darling, but now thank God you are coming home. I often wonder if you still have your signet ring, I have still got your ring darling, and will wear it whenever you want me to.

Goodbye now darling, take great care of yourself, remember my thoughts are with you always.

Your ever loving Sweetheart,
Gladys xxxxxxxxxxxxxxxxxxxxxxx

Bert was moved to a transit camp, in order, he believes to be fattened up a bit, as people would have been too horrified by the sight of so many of the prisoners weighing no more than four or five stones. Finally he boarded SS *Chitral*, calling in at Ceylon, then up through Suez, and on until they anchored off Port Said for fuel. It was there that Bert received his first mail from home in almost four years.

There was a huge pile of letters from Gladys: 'I discovered that she had written sometimes twice a day. Among her many letters, lots being forces airmail, were several ordinary ones, some of which contained photographs of how she now looked at twenty-one – I had last seen her at sixteen. Oh what a difference, and I couldn't stop from looking at them. I placed her letters in chronological order, read and re-read them over again. Later I sat down to answer them. Time wasn't important to me, but when I had finished my over twenty-page reply, I discovered that most everyone had turned in and it was about 3.30am.'

H.M.S. Chitral   64 Walker Road
                                                    Nth Kensington
                                                    London W10

                                                    October 19th, 1945

My Very Own Darling,

Today is one of the days that will live in my memory for ever. For today I received 12 of your letters that you have written to me, the first letters since I was released. There are so many of your letters darling, that I think the best way I can answer them, is to answer them in rotation. This is going to be a long letter dear, but I will do my utmost to answer everything you have asked me.

There is one thing that I regret, and that is, not receiving these letters before. It's not your fault dearest, or anyone's, for I am sure that everything possible has been done to get the mail to us, as quickly as possible. This afternoon we left Port Said, and now we will not have any more stops until we reach Southampton. So you will very likely hear from me before you receive this letter.

Letter 1

Darling, I am so glad to know that my letter brought you so much happiness. I am glad dearest, because they also gave me happiness to write them. I have written several letters since then but unfortunately I didn't know you had changed addresses, and I do so hope that you will get them eventually.

Thank you darling for saving your fourteen days holiday until I get home. Yes dear, we will spend the first seven days with my family, and I am sure that Mum would love you, for can anybody not love such a wonderful woman as you are dear. I am afraid that I don't know what I would like to do, except of course that I want to see all those who are so dear to me. You most of all darling, being the dearest one to me. No my sweet, I am not the type of man to let my wife work. But, before she became my wife, I would make sure that we could live comfortably off my wages before we were married.

Letter 2

It makes me happy to know that I have you waiting for me dearest. Yes darling, I am longing to see you, more than words can express, and it thrills me to know that you are longing to see me. I have received your photographs, and will tell you more in a later page.

Tell your mum that I shall be very happy to come and stay with you at the earliest possible moment. Yes darling I do know that you especially want me to stay with you, it's this knowledge that makes me so happy, you wonderful adorable darling. I shall never forget the things that we used to do for these memories have helped me to keep my 'chin up' during the darkest hours that I have endured, and it was also the fact that I loved you so much, and knew that you loved me, that gave me courage to fight against despair, and eventually win through. You need never fear that my feelings for you have ever altered, and you can rest assured darling, that things are not going to be the same as when I went away, they are going to be even better.

Letter 3

It gives me untold happiness to know that you love my Mother so. I am sure she loves you as much.

Darling, please. How could you ever think that I would ever fall out of love with you. Even if you are grown up, and are twenty one, please darling, always remember this. I love you, I adore you, I always have since I first met you, and will go on doing so, until the end of my life. My dearest one, I hope I have driven that little doubt out of your beautiful head. Please believe me dearest when, I say I love you, on my honour, I do.

I have received five of your photographs, but I want to answer them later for a special reason. You must try and concentrate on your work dear. If you feel excited as I do, I can well realize how you feel, but you must try to concentrate on your work, as I wouldn't want anybody to think that my future wife was incompetent at her work. But you have my sympathy, as I hardly know what I am doing practically all day.

I am glad to be able to say, that I have never felt any fitter in my life. So darling, please do not worry any more, as worry mars beauty and you are very beautiful, my own sweet angel. Remember your own words 'Love always comes out on top.'

Letter 4

Please give my congratulations to the girl who got married to a lad who had been overseas three years. I hope and pray, that you will know that I am still the one for you.

Darling, I do believe you, when you say that you'll always love me, and darling when I get back I'll prove to you that I shall always love you dearest, but don't blame me for the consequences that will follow. (You'll love it darling.)

Darling, I want you to know that I never want anyone but you to help me find my future happiness, and unless I can have you to make me happy, I promise the world that I'll be the unhappiest man living. Will you help me to be happy? I am sure that we could find happiness together darling, just you and I, in a world of our own. I am glad to hear that you will be leaving the N.F.S. darling. If you do get a job it will only be until that happy day when we are in the position to be married.

Letter 5

This is one of my favourite letters from you darling. I am very sorry to say that owing to the terrible food that we got as Ps.O.W., I had to sell my signet ring to enable me to buy fruit and eggs, which I really believe helped me physically to endure what we had to. But I can assure you darling, if I did have my ring I would now be wearing it, ON MY THIRD FINGER, LEFT HAND. As you say my sweet, a ring is really nothing – it's what it stands for. I am so sorry that I haven't got a ring to wear so as I could let the world know that I am engaged to the most sweetest girl in the whole world, and will do anything to make her the husband that she deserves, for the patience and love that she has shown and given to me. You most heavenly angel, you will never regret waiting for me, and as you offer me your whole life, I will take it, but only on condition that you take mine, as I also want you to take my heart as it is yours alone.

Darling you have made me overjoyed to know that you love me so much as to make what is yours, mine as well. I want you to know my sweet that whatever I possess, including my heart is yours darling to do with it what ever you may desire.

Letter 6

I am very sorry to hear that Mr. Norman passed away, as he is part of my never to be forgotten memories. Do you remember how, on the first morning that you called for me, I wasn't awake, and Mr. Norman, came up and woke me, telling me you were downstairs, and that it was eight o'clock. I never moved as fast as I did then. I often smile when I think of it. Do you also remember the night you showed me the back entrance to Mr. and Mrs. Norman's house, and how I was too shy to kiss you goodnight? When I was walking towards the house, I felt as if I could kick myself but then it happened. You called me back. Then you kissed me and hurried home. That night I could hardly sleep and it wasn't with insomnia either. All I could do was to lie there, hugging the pillow and think of our first kiss.

The kiss that was to bind our two lives together forever. When I get home, the word parting for me and you will cease to exist. We have been parted for long enough, and I don't want to ever be away from you again darling.

The question I wanted to ask you has practically been asked but before I complete it, I want you to promise me faithfully darling, that when I get back, and am able to take you in my arms again, you will let me ask you again verbally, as I still think that it should only be spoken as the answer should be given right away.

The question is darling Will you marry me? I want you so much to say yes, but I must tell you that I really want to get a good job before we get married, as I do so want to make our future secure, and would hate myself, if you were made to worry over financial affairs, first because I can't give you the happiness I want to. Admittedly, I shall have quite a little account when I am discharged, but we must have something by for *little things* that are bound to come when two people love each other as we do. I sincerely hope darling, that you will understand my feelings, and see things as I do, I do so much want our future to be a secure one. Please dearest believe me when I say I really love you, and want, more than anything in the world, to make you my wife, but have patience until I can get employment with a pretty solid future. It won't be long and we will never regret waiting that little bit longer. In the mean time I will have you, and you me. Please darling will you wait?

Letter 7

Darling I try hard not to worry over future employment, but as I have explained in my answer to your previous letter my future employment means so much to both of us and our future, but as you insist dear, I'll try even harder to stop worrying, but I tell you, every time I think of you dear, I automatically think of our marriage, and then I can't but think of employment. I cannot possibly have a good rest when I get home because I shall be with you dearest, and even to think of you makes my heart beat twice as fast, and if the doctor knew, I am sure he would order me a nice long holiday, and so, already knowing the Dr.s remedy, I shan't go to him, but (I) (sorry darling) *we* are going to have a holiday *together*. (By the way you are giving me orders before we are married aren't you?, and I love it.)

To read your letters and know that you love me very much can only be beaten by one thing, hearing you tell me yourself Gladys darling, and I can faithfully say that I really do love you and long to be with you, to put my arms around you, kiss you and hear you say 'Albert, I love you.' To see you sign yourself 'your ever loving and devoted Fiancee' makes me feel as if I have had a charge of electricity passed into my body, I am tingling all over.

Letter 8

I am so glad that you look forward to my letters so much. I am sorry I haven't written more, but until I arrive in England, they will have to be limited owing to weight, as they go by air. I should like to see all the old letters I have sent you. I had all yours up to capitulation, but when the island fell, everything was in a turmoil, and I lost everything, except two photographs of you and one or two others.

I shall be overjoyed to come and stay with you all, and I am looking forward to seeing your new home. If you like it, I'm sure I shall.

Yes darling, as Mum said, you must get ready for your holiday, heaven knows you have waited long enough for it, but I promise you faithfully darling that it will be the happiest you or I have ever had. How well I remember that night that we were alone in the house together, but I also remember what a fool I was. There was I with a beautiful girl on my knee, a girl who loved me, and all I could do was nothing. I'm sorry I was so shy darling, but we will make up for all that when I get back. Darling prepare yourself for a bombardment of love as you have never experienced before (Whew! was that me?)

The thought, that you love me dear, is constantly in my mind all day and night. You are my dreams come true, you are my own fairy princess, my own sleeping beauty whom I shall awaken into a new life, that we will share together my darling.

Letter 9

I am terribly sorry that my letter you received dated Sept. 30th upset you so, I don't know what could have come over me to write such a dull letter. You know my darling Gladys to cause you upset or worry is the last thing I would ever want to do in this world. You are the only one that I ever want to share life with. With you I am sure I shall soon get back to a normal way of living.

Gladys Darling please help me out of a brain muddle. I have read in your ninth letter that I know how much you long to be the one who makes me my partner in life, but I must love you really and truly to ask you to be my wife. Oh Gladys, dearest beloved sweetheart, please tell me that you never doubted my love not for one single second, tell me that you know I love you. Tell me darling these things I want to know, and my darling, please say you will be my wife. I love you so much darling, that to think that you ever doubted my word, is like a knife thrust into my heart. Please tell me I have misunderstood your letter.

I mentioned previously that I had received your photos, but wanted to say something on another page well here it is. You have altered a little in appearance, but darling you have altered as a rose alters. The bud of a rose when young, is beautiful, but when that rose is fully bloomed into all its glory it is different in appearance, but darling, it is more beautiful. Yes my love I really mean it, you were beautiful when I first fell in love with you, and now you have blossomed into a woman, you are even more beautiful. If I remember, you always wanted to be a bit taller, and I shall love to have you as you are. Yes dear, all these years that we could have been together, maybe as man and wife, have been taken from us but we will make up for it ten-fold when I get back, which cannot come too quickly for me either. Gladys darling, it brings me untold happiness to know that you love me heart and soul and I love you the same darling. You say you will be to me what I want you to be. I want you to be my loving wife, to share my life forever, please darling keep your promise and say, *I will*.

Whatever made you think that I would only want you as a friend and not a wife. Darling please tell me that you did not mean it, in the way I think you might.

Letter 10

Again I have to apologise for disturbing your mind with my gloomy letters, but I honestly think that I am doing right in thinking of our future dear. Of course I love you darling, and am very glad to know that you think we can make a go of it, right from the start. It's the same as I think, and I am building my dreams darling just as you want me to do, knowing as I do, that I have someone like you to return to after work each day, would make life as pleasant as anyone could wish for. *I love you*.

You wonder if I shall still think of you as I did so long ago. You know I do darling, don't you? You have changed a bit dearest, but I still see you as I left you, as someone who loves me and someone whom I deeply love heart, body and soul. This is the last letter I have to answer at present, and so I think I must order you about before we are married. I have noticed in your letters that you seem to fear that I shall not love you as I did when I went away. You mustn't worry any more darling. I have tried to convince you that I really and truly do love you darling. I only hope that you believe me dear. So please my dearest one do not worry anymore, trust me, and we will be trusting each other. I am sure that we will make an excellent husband and wife, and may I say parents?

You ask me if I remember Beryl. How could I forget her. If it hadn't been for her we might never have known what real love was. No darling I shall never forget Beryl's letter in June 1940. 'My young cousin would like to write to someone in the forces.' No, I shall never forget Beryl, she brought you to me and that is something I shall ever be grateful to her for doing.

Darling you ask me if your letters have made me happy. Gladys my dearest own, the moment I received your letters and photographs I was the happiest man in the world. So happy was I that I got several curious glances, as I walked along the deck smiling to myself, perhaps they thought I was a little crazy, but they were wrong, I'm not a little crazy I'm completely crazy about you darling and everything I wanted to know or hear was in your letters. The lads tell me not to look at your photograph as much, I will wear it out with my eyes. You ask me to remember you darling. How could I ever forget you dear. You mean so much to me that I don't think I could live without you, so please don't ask me to try, I would never survive the ordeal.

We have been told that we should arrive at Southampton on Sunday week and disembark on Monday. How true this is I don't know but by the time you receive this letter I should be in England, and will have sent you a telegram. We have also been told that we will very likely go to a camp for one or two days, and then our leave starts.

As I have mentioned before in this letter, I shall take your advice and spend the first seven days in and around home, with you of course dearest, and then we must go and see your people dear. As we are going to spend the first seven days in London, I think it best for you to come there. I will let you know the exact date as soon as possible, so as you can arrange your leave, and then you can let me know what time train you are catching and when it will arrive. Oh

Darling, I can hardly wait for that day when we are together again. For so long have I looked forward to this journey, and the people I was to see again when it was finished. Now the journey is nearly over, I can hardly wait to set foot on English soil again, but most of all are the dear ones whom I love, and who are waiting there to welcome me home. Gladys darling, you are the dearest one who is waiting for me, and I love you so, that I cannot explain it on paper, but will have to wait to show you how much I really love you, dearest Gladys.

And so I must draw to a close, I don't know when you will receive this letter, but when you do, I want you to know darling, that I mean every word of it. Especially that I want you to be my wife. Give my love to all at home.

To you my dearest one, I send my undying love and devotion, knowing that our future together dear is going to be everything that we wish it to be. Because you love me, and I love you darling, and will always be your ever loving,

Albert xxxxxxxxxxxxxxxxxxxxxxxxxxxxxxxxxxxxxxxxxxxxxxxxxxxx
xxxxxxxxxxxx
xxxxxxxxxxxxxxxxxxxxxxxxxxxxxxxxxxxxxxxxxxxxxxxxxxxxxxxxxxxx
xxxxxxxxxxxx
P.S. You're beautiful
darling. xxxxxxxxxxxxxxxxxxxxxxxxxxxxxxxxxxxxxxxxxxxxxxxxx

On 23 September, Gladys had written to Bert, allowing herself the luxury of really beginning to anticipate his return and their reunion:

Our meeting again will remind us of the first time we met won't it dear, but this time of course so very much more has happened and time has passed, which we have got to make up for. I am still in love with you as I was nearly five years ago, I hope you haven't forgotten all the things we used to do dearest, and that there is still a place for me in your heart. It is such a long time ago that you were able to say you loved me, and in the few years that have gone

I have grown up, but I still long for you dear, I hope that everything is going to be as it was before you went away, but must wait still a tiny while longer.

Goodbye for a while then darling Albert, oh darling, by the way, when you arrive in England and if you are able to, and wish to get in touch with me quickly on all odd dates in October, and even dates in November you could telephone me at Bridgwater 2485 . . .

Three days later she finally heard from him, and wrote back immediately. Knowing what Bert was alluding to in his letter of 14 September 1945 when he wrote 'and one day I have a question to ask you', Gladys, in questioning him about their plans for his return, says boldly,

So darling please tell me what you would like to do. Of course you will get a lot more days than 14 darling, I can only have 14 unless of course we get married and then I would have 28 days. Are you the type of fellow who wouldn't allow his wife to work? Do tell me all these things darling.

It must have been difficult, if not impossible, for Gladys to realize quite the scale of adjustment Bert was in the process of making from prisoner-of-war to civilian. He hints at it in his letter to her dated 30 September 1945:

I try and plan our future together darling, but my dreams all seem to tumble to dust when I realize how life has changed since I was taken P.O.W. Every day I read the news sheets, but my mind is in constant turmoil, trying to piece things together. It's just like a gigantic jigsaw puzzle with several key pieces missing. It's just like being born into a new world and learning to live all over again . . .

There is so much I have forgotten during those dark three and a half years, that I often wonder if I have a memory left at all. I have never forgotten that I love you darling, or that you have been waiting patiently and faithfully for my return. I shall always see

that as a great sacrifice on your part darling, and will try my utmost
to repay you.

Meanwhile Gladys's last letters to Bert were full of hope and
excitement.

'Ye Olde Oak Inne'
20 High Street
Bridgwater
Somerset

27-9-45

My Darling Albert,

Today I have read your letters over and over again as if for the first
time every time, it's so marvellous to have mail from you my dear,
and I am longing for more.

I am glad your Mum and Rita spoke well of me – we have
written to each other regularly and found immense pleasure from
doing so. We understand each other darling and I also call your
mother 'Mum Read', she's so very nice to me darling, I love her
like my own mother.

It thrills me to know that you are still in love with me, I wonder
if you really will now that I am 'grown up', I was 21 last May 5th
darling, so you see that is a little bit of difference isn't it? Darling I
want you to love me so much, because we could make so much of
our lives together, and I am still very much in love with you.

I hope you have had all the photographs I have sent you, please
let me know, and if you like my plans for our holiday together, I
am getting very excited about it all my darling, it is such a great
big relief to know that you are safe and coming home, dear Albert
how you deserve all the kindness and love that we can give you, I
hope and pray my darling that I never hurt you in any way,
physically or mentally.

Darling I hope you come home soon, I cannot put my mind to
my work, or concentrate on anything, you live in my thoughts
continually. So darling chin up, a little more waiting and we shall

be together for ever, so as I close now dear I say, goodbye, goodnight and God bless you darling, please get in touch with me as soon as you can, I am so afraid of wasting a few minutes. Darling, please tell me in your next letter if you feel well, it worries me. Bye, Bye now, love always comes out on top dear.
God bless you again.

All my fondest love and devotion

Always your beloved,
Gladys xxxxxxxxxxxxxxxxxxxxxxxxxxxxxxxxxxxxxxxxxxxxxxxxxxx

> Old Oak Inne
> 20 High Street
> Bridgwater
> Somerset
>
> 30-9-45

My Own Darling Albert,

I have a very crazy feeling dear that makes me want to shut myself away from everyone and do nothing but write to you, I know you will not mind if I put my heart on paper to you. Remember to let me know when you have my photographs darling. Albert, I meant to ask you before darling have you got the signet ring still, if you have darling what finger of what hand do you wear it, I have often wondered about it, and on what finger do you wish me to wear your ring darling. Albert darling, are you really very pleased when you had my letter which said I will always wear your ring, rings are really nothing darling, but it is what they stand for and mean that really counts. My wearing your ring on my third finger left hand means to an outsider that I am engaged, but to me my darling it not only means I am engaged but that I belong to the best and dearest fellow on earth, one that I love very very much and one to whom I shall give my whole life to.

Darling do you have any idea of when you will be home? I am so longing for you to return to me. In your letter dear you said we shall have many ups and downs in life, that may be very true but my own darling with you beside me for ever, we can face all the future has to give. Can I send you anything my dearest please let me know? Cigarettes etc. don't be afraid to ask for anything, all of mine dear is yours also. Now my darling once more I draw to a close, every day a day nearer our being together for ever. Goodbye my darling, and God bless, I have now your photograph with me always and have done so for all the time you have been away, during which time I had no mail darling but my thoughts were then as they are now dear always with you. *I love you* very very much my darling, and want you with me always. I will be to you darling, as you to me, always your loving and devoted sweetheart,

Gladys xxxxxxxxxxxxxxxxxxxxxxxxxxxxxxxxxxxx
I do hope you are well and getting strong my darling.
Bye Bye now.
Always yours
Gladys xxxxxxxxxxxxx

Old Oak Inn
20 High Street
Bridgwater
Somerset

19-10-45

My Own Darling Albert,

Another two days and no letter darling so I really believe you are well on the way home now, oh Albert my dearest I am so excited and so very happy for you. I have written a letter to you and sent it to your Mum to keep and let you have when you get home, as I think you may not get these I have written.

Well darling I hope you are well and very happy and looking forward to our years of life and love together. Yes darling we will talk over our future together, and lots of other things when you get back, there is so much we have to say to one another, and I am longing to see you and be with you for ever and ever.

I shall always love and adore you my dearest, and hope that I shall never cause you any hurt. When you come home darling never

never let us part. I want to be with you always, for I love you, and
it has been so long.

Goodbye now darling, take great care of yourself and come to
me darling I shall always be waiting.

Goodbye. God bless you darling.
Always for ever, your loving,
Gladys xxxxxxxxxxxxxxxxxxxxxxxxxxxxxxxxxxxxx

The following afternoon, Bert arrived at Paddington Station to meet
Gladys's train: 'The time seemed to drag by but then I could see the train
approaching in the distance as it slowly slid into the platform to stop with
a loud squealing of brakes. Doors were thrown open, crowds began to
emerge in a thronging mass. Would I see her? Would she see me? And
then I spotted a small figure at the far end of the train, worried look upon
her lovely face. She looked up, I waved frantically. She saw me and waved
back. I had recognized her, she me! It seemed ages as she made her way
towards the barrier, then we were only feet apart. I had always been so
shy, but that seemed so long ago, as we flung our arms about each other
hugging and kissing as if no one else mattered. We were together again
at last. That was so many years ago now, but we still feel the same towards
each other.'

Bert and Gladys finally got married on 17 January 1946. They have
three sons. Gladys has kept every single letter Bert ever wrote to her. Bert
can't remember ever actually asking Gladys to marry him, they just knew
it would happen. Bert refers to Gladys as his 'strength'. 'I could never
imagine life without her.'

The POW camps left their mark on Bert. He has never truly got over
them. He is, however, happy to be reminded of what he and Gladys were
to each other in those days and they still listen to 'their' song, 'Deep
Purple'. He is now in a wheelchair, but always used to sit at Gladys's feet
and read their letters aloud. They are a bit of his past that he would rather
not forget.

BOB &
DOT GRAFTON

Bob and Dot joined the Roding Road Club, quite by chance, on the same day in 1938. They were both sixteen, living in Manor Park, a poor part of the East End of London, and were keen cyclists.

The cycling club made a habit of stopping off at roadside cafés and listening to music. Dot remembers their first excursion with the club: 'Bob, being a gentleman, asked me what I'd like. That was it, we rode together for fifty years. We went camping with the club, but there was no hanky-panky, there was that respect there. The boys went in the boys' tent, the girls in the girls' tent. We slept together, but we didn't make love until we got married.'

On 8 May 1941, Bob left the bookshop at which he was working for the Royal Artillery. By then he was nineteen. He spent three months training in radar before he was sent overseas. He and Dot wrote to each other frequently but, at that stage, neither could have anticipated the separation they were about to endure. They were separated for four years and for two of them Bob was missing. Dot continued to write to him throughout. All her letters were 'returned to sender', but her mother, anxious to make Dot feel that some had got through, burned many of them.

Bob's last letter to Dot before embarkation tenderly but surely and convincingly persuades Dot of his certainty in their relationship.

Yes, darling, I know that you will wait for me. Darling do you know this. I swear that as long as we are apart I will never touch another woman either physically or mentally.

A promise. A declaration. Something for Dot to hold on to over the four years of separation that were to follow.

L/Bde Grafton R W

Saturday 07.9.41

My Dearest Darling Dorothy,

This my darling, is a very sad moment when the realisation of the fact that, now there is no hope of us seeing each other again for

Saturday Oct 13th 1945

My Dearest Darling Sweetest Bob,

I just had to write one more letter to you to say with all my heart & soul "Welcome Home" in those two words I wish to convey to you all the love & devotion I possess. With all the sincerity I can give darling I mean that, I have lived these past four years for this time to come and now it is nearly here and am just aching to see you.

You will never know how much you have been in my thoughts love, honestly they have been constantly with you, often I have sat down to a lovely meal & have thought "I wonder what my Bob is having to eat" my meal has gone untouched. Not once but hundreds of times I have cried myself to sleep thats just two little incidents there are lots more dear. I tell you these because I do so want you to realise that its YOU only YOU that makes my life & now the time has come when we can start planning our life as we want it & put all our dreams into practice.

So love those two small words mean a whole "world" to me & you.

Everyone at home is thinking of you just waiting to welcome you back. Friends have enquired about you on numerous occasions or tell me to convey to you the best luck in the world.

Darling I do hope you are able to phone us, that would help a lot. I do hope those last few hours of your journey pass quickly & when the train shunts in will be waiting, so look out for us won't you dear.

Until then I wish you "Gods Speed", and send you, as I have told you so many many times all my love, just a little while longer & I'll feel the touch of my Bobs lips after four years, whats a lovely thought.

Good night darling, god bless & heres to that first kiss with loveads some time, slowly dawns upon me. I find it leaves me a little numb and very miserable. As you have so often told me we must make the best of the circumstances thrust upon us. I thank God for your letter dated September 23rd honey. I realised more than ever Dot, the depth and sincerity of your feelings. I know more than ever how much you love me and how much I love you. Darling believe me when I say how much I cling to it. Circumstances, parades, etc., having left me only with this afternoon in which to write to you darling for the last time until the ship *sails*. Then my letters will be censored as this one possibly will be. I have very little information myself darling as to what exactly is happening, so there is very little that I can tell you. This I do know honey that we are going to embark on arrival at the port. There has been a flurry of final preparations which left us in a whirlwind. I had to stay two nights at Whitsands Bay because of a wet thick sea mist which made it impossible to drive a lorry along the cliffs. Darling for the moment I am going to forget the fact that I am off and am firstly going to answer all your letters one by one to date. It cheers me up.

I wasn't surprised about Tommy and Daphne really honey were you? I really did not think that it would last very long as they never seemed settled did they. I have not heard from Addy since he went into hospital. I hope he is going along OK. I was told though that he wrote to one of the fellows on the entertainment committee about the next show, which of course I won't see as it is on Monday. Apparently he has the same outside turns as before, Tap dancers aged from a cute little girl of 9 years to young women. They are quite good. I shall 'phone you tonight honey. 2414. Darling I am sorry I mentioned about money but I guess I got the wrong idea Eh! So darling you can rest assured that I have no regrets whatever for making that allowance. I am quite happy about it. Fancy granny catching you on the hop like that darling. I could imagine it and it made me laugh.

Yes darling I *know* that you will wait for me. Darling do you know this. I swear that as long as we are apart I will never never touch another woman either physically or mentally. I do mean that Dot an awful lot. I got quite a large amount of letters here which I have packed in one of my kit bags. I shall take those with me where ever I go Dot. Each day I shall read one of them so that I might always have a letter from you every day. I carry with me darling so many tender memories which I treasure. Our day will come, never fear Dot. Darling you are so encouraging. I expect before this war is through I will be remembering those words of yours about being lonely. I shall know darling that your thoughts and prayers are with me as mine are always with you. I know you'll be good Dot. If I thought otherwise I'd find some way of not going. If you really think you could wait 20 years honey I know then that you can wait at the most 20 months. I got a lot from that letter darling and I can always turn to it when I feel low. Please darling don't ever talk about if I want to be free. Never darling. I want you more than anything in the world. We were meant to belong to each other Dot. These few months we have been parted have proved to me more than ever how true it is. And honey as you say 'One half of me has died.' I can honestly say darling that not for one little moment has my attention been taken by any other girl. That is the path I shall always follow, no matter what happens. Don't ever ever doubt me Dot, if you did it would honestly be an injustice. I did mean that Dot about I'd rather you dead than have anyone lay a finger on you in the form of a loving caress. Funny thing darling how strong love can grow. As I told your mum in my letter, that even if I have not much at the moment, you will never want from me not trying or doing my best. I want you to be happy more than *ANYTHING* in the world Dot. Don't let this upset you too much honey please. Many times have I seen those big blue eyes filled with tears but when I ask you to smile you have through the tears. Do it again darling even though I can't see you smiling. That's the most radiant sunshine ever is your smile. Darling things have happened so very quickly that I have only time to write one letter tonight. I wrote to mum very shortly in a few spare moments but I don't think that I explained that I would be embarking so quickly. If darling you don't hear from me for a few days please don't worry as we are not allowed to write, phone or leave from the port until the convoy actually sails. John is John Ives. Ken says thank you very much for the kiss, one day he hopes to reciprocate personally. He also says not to worry he will take good care of me.

Please when you see mum explain to her for me darling. Give my best wishes to everyone darling. Darling I had some more to say but they have got me another job to do. God be with you and yours always darling and take care of you for me.

I will write to you just as soon as I get a few moments. Darling I will phone you tonight and it seems funny to think that I will pass through London en route for the port.

Well darling I write again as soon as possible.

Always remember we are part of each other.

I shall always remain
Yours Ever
With love and Devotion so deep that the fires burn even in sleep.
Bob
xxxxxxxxxxxxxxxxxxxxxxxxxxxxxxxxxxx
xxxxxxxxxxxxxxxxxxxxxxxxxxxxxxxxxxx and 100,000,000,000 more

P.S. Enclosed post card reminder of Whitsands Bay where one day we might even spend our honeymoon.

Dot received Bob's letters from the ship, and one from Singapore, but after that there was silence. After Singapore fell, he had escaped in a junk, which got becalmed and stuck. Bob swam to an island, and with three friends bartered with the inhabitants for a boat. They quickly became sunburned and almost indistinguishable from the islanders. They went from island to island, and finally arrived in Sumatra, which had fallen the day before. There they met up with Captain Apthorpe, who was in charge of the British Sumatran Battalion, a mixture of men from the Army, the Navy and the Air Force, who had been formed into one unit. Bob referred to the unit as the 'roughs and toughs'. Bob, a lance bombardier, found Captain Apthorpe very strict, but very fair. 'He had to mould those men.'

At the beginning of March 1942 they were captured by the Japanese. They were forced to build their camp and then a railway. Bob wrote to Dot twice a week, but she received nothing until 1944, when the statutory twenty-five words arrived telling her merely that he was alive and well, and a prisoner-of-war.

Looking back, Dot says, 'I always thought he'd come home, I wouldn't dare think anything else.'

The first letter to reach Dot arrived in September 1945, which Bob had sent in August from a jungle camp in Indo-China. It was written on lavatory paper. Once he was on his way home, Bob continued to write to Dot, but he didn't receive any of her final air letters to him until after he had returned and they were man and wife.

Despite the extreme hardship that Bob had endured since he had last seen Dot four years before, he pays tribute simply, yet movingly, in the following letter to her role as being the most difficult:

At Sea

Dorothy Mine,

It's almost 4 years ago now since I was on another such ship. The difference was of course that every hour we drew farther and farther apart. Now darling, every hour seems a day because I know that we are at the end of my journeying. I spend the day in the way that suits the mood. Mostly reading. So that when night comes I am tired and do not lie awake these long hours with my brain racing away at top speed thinking and thinking over things which at one time I thought would never come true. When I wake in the morning I always think of the miles the ship has throbbed through during the quiet sleeping hours of night. And when I think of that I am glad because that is 8 hrs over which I need not be impatient, they passed easily and without my knowing.

Does it seem four years to you darling? To me it might almost be the same ship and I have forgotten to get off. This time of course my heart is light and not burdened. Yet that which I thought would burn and rankle with bitter hatred, already begins to fade in the light of new hopes and happiness. Except in occasional nightmares in which I am always prevented from reaching you by a Jap.

This I know, that it was you of the two of us who had the more difficult task. For I am a man (perhaps prematurely) and men must fight and women must weep. So my share was no exception, yours was. So faithful Dorothy as I have not wings I wait patiently and find solace in my thoughts. Even if we have lost four years we'll make life so that it is never regretted.

If darling there is anything in this mind over matter business then you can expect to see this ship land in the playground anytime.

I love you.
Your Bob

1st October, 1945

My Dearest Sweetheart,

I imagine that this will be the last letter in this series as being very near our next port of call the mail bag is open. I reckon that by the time the calendar has ticked off 17 days I'll be there in your arms. By the time you've read this my darling it will be less than a fortnight. Oh Dot until I hear your voice so comforting and look into your eyes I shall not be cut off from the sordid revolting life of the past or even the bad dreams I seem to have lately. Until 4 o'c last night my love, I lay trying to imagine just what you would do when we first see each other again and just what you'd say. Darling all through my memories of you have kept themselves dear and like a goal or prize to win or bust. And though I know not why you should have waited for me, I never for one moment ever doubted. Some of the lads couldn't understand this, seeing that I didn't hear from you until Aug. 4th. They used to say of course the girl won't wait. But I knew. It has not been hard for me, but for you darling it must have been. Seeing that there must have been thousands of attractive and eligible young men in England all through. I know darling that you will not think me high hat if I say to myself then she might love me. For Dot I loved you so much I am sure you might have felt it sometime. I feel certain that I shall pick up some mail from you in P.S. which believe me will brighten up this trip for me immensely and give me something to think about. A few letters will make all that difference. Do you remember darling a letter which you wrote to me at Plymouth which you very sweetly devoted entirely to imagining what a honeymoon would be like. I remember it well for I read it many times and loved it together with a lock of hair, both yours and 'Mary's' remember. I kept them in my wallet together with some 100 photos of home, holidays and you (in a bathing costume) and Ruth's wedding. I had the misfortune of losing the whole lot. At that time I was able to vent some of my anger on the Nips for losing it. Later I grew more and more sorry I'd had that misfortune. Still a little longer and I can see you in person again. Just lay back Dot darling and think of all the things you'd like to do and places you'd like to go and we'll do and go.

All my love,
Your Bob

Dot brushes off Bob's tribute to her courage and faithfulness, in this letter:

Monday 1st October, 1945

Hello Honey,

Here I am again – still sitting in front of the fire drying my hair.

Darling you tell me I have been courageous and faithful waiting this long while for you to return, not only you but friends at the office marvel at my patience and sincerity but honestly darling how can I make you understand that I have not been heroic or anything, I love you and with these three words I mean that I just live to be in your company, you are my aim in life, my desire and like others I have no desire for anyone else, no others company would please me, I would not enjoy it, I have no interest or desire to be more than just a friend to others. I am sure dear that I astonished my Mother and Father, I really think they thought that when you were out of sight you would be out of mind, but they have realised how wrong they were. I was, I agree, a flirt I suppose you would call it when I first knew you dear, you thought you would teach me a thing or two do you remember, well you did dear. I think I would even have surprised you love if you knew how quiet I became when you went away. Half of me had gone but it left behind a different Dot, a girl who wanted to do nothing to stop her Bobby from loving her. I made sure that I did all within my power to show, or try to convey to you how much I think and pray for you. I had very little opportunities of showing you, the only way I could do it was writing to you as much as possible but other powers beyond our control would not even allow my letters through. Lots of people here have told me 'you are wasting your time, you are only young once, go out and enjoy yourself, have a good time', but I know my Bob and I made my choice and thank goodness all is coming right at last. I wonder how many people there are who made fools of themselves, not one but hundreds. Funny Bob I am weak willed in some things but others no. I know what I want and nothing will make me do otherwise. One thing I have done that my Bob does not agree with, but I feel sure under the circumstances you will not mind. I smoke dear as every girl does these days, but dear I do not cough else then I wouldn't. With air raids and things I have found it has done me good – am I forgiven dear – I hope so, although I must tell you very often it has passed through my mind that you are not very keen on my doing it – it has worried me because I just do not want to do anything that will cause me to lose your love and affection, that will kill me honest it would. Still when my Bob comes home he can have my share as cigarettes are pretty scarce these days 'under the counter' for regular customers although they are going to be more plentiful.

Yes dear I know Charlie is with you because I have been in to see Charlie's people and also your Mum goes in there. As a matter of fact I got Charlie's address to write to him but then heard that he had been moved and when his Dad went to send him a telegram, he was told he could not send it, so I have not written. I also knew that Ken had been liberated when I went round home yesterday your Dad had had a very nice letter from Ken's people telling him Ken had been liberated from Saigon.

By the way love your letter was censored even if they said it was not going to be and was posted at Colombo I think, stamp mark dated the 24th and your cable I had from you was dated 23rd from Colombo. It is funny I have to sit and read all the news out to the family when I get letters from you and tonight I rather wanted to know what you had written and I said there was no news, anyway I told them one or two things and let them guess the rest.

No dear I have not heard the Army name for the men who have lived without clothes for over three years. I have not had anything to do with the services – I remember my Bob's warning. I have only seen our friends and they wouldn't tell me.

I do sincerely trust you got some letters from me at Colombo but am wondering as once again you repeated your address on the telegram from Colombo whether you did get some. I am hoping that you sent that telegram off as soon as you arrived and received some mail before you left. More on another Aero.

Lots & Lots of Love dear,
Dot

On Saturday 13 October 1945, Dot wrote not one, but two last letters to Bob, before his arrival back in England on the *Worcestershire*, which docked in Liverpool on the following Monday. This is the final, final letter.

Saturday October 13th 1945

My Dearest Darling Sweetest Bob,

I just had to write one more letter to you to say with all my heart and soul 'Welcome Home' in these two words I wish to convey to you all the love and devotion I possess. With all the sincerity I can give darling, I mean that, I have lived these past four years for this time to come and now it is nearly here and I am just aching to see you.

You will never know how much you have been in my thoughts love, honestly they have been constantly with you, often I have sat down to a lovely meal and have thought 'I wonder what my Bob is having to eat', my meal has gone untouched. Not once but hundreds of times I have cried myself to sleep, that's just two little incidents, there are lots more dear. I tell you these because I do so want you to realize that its YOU only YOU that makes my life and now the time has come when we can start planning our life as we want it and put all our dreams into practice.

So love those two small words mean a whole 'world' to me and you.

Everyone at home is thinking of you just waiting to welcome you back. Friends have enquired about you on numerous occasions and tell me to convey to you the best luck in the world.

Darling, I do hope you are able to phone us, that would help a lot. I do hope those last few hours of your journey pass quickly and when the train shunts in we'll be waiting, so look out for us won't you dear.

Until then I wish you God's Speed, and send you, as I have told you so many many times, all my love, just a little while longer and I'll feel the touch of my Bobs lips after four years, what a lovely thought.

Good night darling, god bless and here's to that first kiss with hundreds to follow.

Yours for ever and ever.

I love you with all my heart, and once again a great big welcome home.

Until then — sweet dreams darling,
Dotty xxxxxxxxxxxxxxxxxxxxxxxxxxxx
xxx? (for Jim)
hundreds more

The day the boat docked, Bob's parents came round to Dot's parents' house, to await his telephone call. She remembers his first words, 'Aren't you cockney?' and then feeling both overwhelming relief and quietly happy. She was lost for words but, surrounded by family as she was, it was difficult to talk anyway.

Throughout the four years' separation, Dot had been teased by friends and family that she would go off with a Yank. 'I'm no angel, but I waited. Bob was a rather special person. I say that not just because he was my husband, but because everyone said so. When he'd gone I was as miserable as miserable. At night I cried and cried. I was one of the biggest flirts out, but the moment I set eyes on Bob, that was that. He was sure I'd still be there, even though I was only a kid. To me the four years away were very important. We'd always said we'd marry at twenty-one and have two kids. Before he went we saw each other every day. Four years did something to our relationship, it's why it was so successful. I felt nearer to him by writing the letters. I always hoped – that is what kept me going. The fact that he was away so long cemented my feelings. I said I'd never marry if he didn't come home. We were reunited on Paddington Station at five in the morning. He got out of the train at the exact spot on the platform where I was standing. We could hardly speak for the first day and night.'

Before their wedding, Bob wrote one last letter to Dot. In it he speaks of the changed nature of their love, its ripening, its maturing, and how the horror of the last four years has only been cleansed and assuaged by the contemplation of his 'wife to be'.

Nov. 1945

My Darling Wife, to be,

It struck me today just how much you must trust me to consent to place your whole life and future in my hands for me to model and shape. If you think about it you see how our separate lives become one and that all which effects one in future will effect the other.

I've written you many letters in which my darling I have tried to impress upon you that I love you. Now after such a prolonged absence from you I often wonder at the fact that the love I had for you before could enlarge to the extent that it has now. I know I used to ache inside because I loved you so much. Now darling, it has gone beyond that. I am sure you too have seen the vast difference in our relationship. It has become far more trusting, deeper and steady as a rock.

I know my sweet that I am not always on my best behaviour but Dot I am still amazed that we have managed to be as good as we have.

It is easy to sit here now, so quiet and peaceful and be able to write 20 pages on the whys and wherefores that make me love you more than anything in the whole world. I shall confine it to saying darling that my knowledge of women begins and ends with Dot. It will always be that way. Sometimes Dot when I have the opportunity of looking at you quietly, I get a feeling that I want to go on my knees and worship you. It all starts from something deep down inside, something inexplicable. Unless you read this when you are quiet you will not take it quite as I mean it.

As I mentioned the other day darling I used to think that I could never feel clean enough to touch you again let alone sleep with you. Not because we had good honest grime on us, that washes off, but because I felt soiled inside from contact with such an awful existence. Therefore darling I kept you in my minds eye as an ideal to get back to. Someone who could make me feel clean and respectable again, someone who has a soft touch, kind eyes, a sweet smile, and chiefly one who has soft words of love, kindness and sympathy which are food and medicine to a man.

So darling you realize that if I had so much as touched another woman out there I don't think I could ever have come back and touched you again. It would have been an indelible stain on my conscience which would never have washed clean.

Dot, my sweet my sole aim in life is to make you happy. Remember it for I won't forget.

Once again last night you would not let me sleep. Before I went to sleep I moved over and made room for you and tried to imagine you there so soft and warm and smooth. I put out a hand and was disappointed. Ah well! I get things revolving and maybe it will come true this most impossible thing. So long my darling I shall always be your most loving husband,

Bob

Bob and Dot were happily married with two sons until Bob's death.

Since filming with Dot early in January, I received a letter from her in which she writes about the immediate period surrounding Bob's illness and death. It seems right to end with that part of her letter:

I think you perhaps would like to hear the end of our story, which as you know started in 1938 when we were both sixteen. Bob developed bone cancer in the hip area, it took months and months to diagnose as everything from a trapped nerve to sciatica was looked into and so of course the pain got worse and the possibility of surgery was out of the question by that stage. In the last stages Bob was in a wheelchair unable to walk. He had a number of spells in hospital for scans and cobalt treatment, but was mostly at home. I would wash and dress him and he would shave himself with his electric razor and never took to his bed until the day before he died and that was only because his doctor said, 'Bob why don't you get into your pyjamas and lie in your bed you will feel so much more comfortable,' and so of course Bob did. Even during the last week of Bob's life I took him out to lunch three times, the last being on the Friday as he died the following Monday. We would arrive at the restaurant at the Masonic Hall and two burly men would come out and lift his wheelchair up the two steps. I did all I could to divert his mind away from the pain despite all the drugs he took. His prisoner of war friends were absolutely great they used to ring him up and chat to him, they rang from all over England, it helped him no end.

The doctor told me he had never seen such a deterioration in a patient over the period of two days as he saw in Bob. The next day Monday 16th May 1988 as Bob lay resting in his bed, our life together ended as it had begun. That spark became a flame that burned furiously for fifty years, and as in life when we always held hands when out together, we were still holding hands as Bob slipped away. As Bob has inscribed in my wedding ring 'Until death do us part'.

Bob was 66 years and 10 months when he died. But we had a great life with the two boys who brought us so much fun and happiness, but the love we had for the boys was nothing to the love we shared together and once the boys went off to University at 18 years of age, Bob and I really began to live. I have no regrets whatsoever, I was so lucky, we had the most marvellous life despite all the tropical illness Bob had to endure. A most caring, loving unselfish man with a great sense of humour and in the last year of his life a very brave man. I could not wish Bob back to continue enduring all that pain. I miss him terribly and always will. Our two sons have their Dad's temperament and both of them with their families are always there when I need support. What more could I expect from life and I am a much better person for having shared my life with Bob.

JACK &
MARY NEWTON

In 1933, the Sutherland family, including their fourteen-year-old daughter Mary, moved to St John's Wood, London. Mr Sutherland was a chauffeur and was given accommodation behind the 'big house'. A few doors down lived the Newtons. Mr Newton was also a chauffeur. They had a son, Jack, who was also fourteen.

'Jack was the boy next door,' says Mary Newton. 'Our families became friends and so did Jack and I. We knew from the beginning that we were the only ones for each other.'

They started courting. By the time Jack joined the RAF Volunteer Reserve in 1938, they knew that they would always be together. Jack went to Maidenhead to the No. 13 Elementary Reserve Flying Training School, where he survived a plane crash, and a year later joined the RAF as a rear gunner on Wellington bombers. He was stationed in Lincolnshire and was called up in 1939. His squadron was known as the 'Thirteen Bar One'.

Throughout this period and during the Blitz, Mary worked at the post office in Cannon Street, in the City of London. Even though she is now seventy-five, Mary still works part-time in her village post office.

On 19 April 1941, Primrose Day, Jack and Mary got married. 'Every year since he has still given me a small bunch of primroses . . . It was a typical wartime wedding; my lace dress cost £3-10s. The cake had a white cardboard cover. There was no real icing because sugar was rationed. And the restaurant where we had the reception had all its windows broken, because of an earlier raid.' They went to the Cotswolds for a four-day honeymoon, staying with friends.

Three months after the wedding on the August bank holiday weekend Mary went up to Lincolnshire to see Jack for three days. They had a 'grand time' and Mary left on the Tuesday morning to return to work. Jack wrote on Tuesday evening:

I cannot thank you enough sweet, for the lovely time you gave me and I only hope I made you feel as happy as you made me feel.

Mary wrote to Jack on the same night:

It won't be long dearest, another fortnight and you'll be home. I'm always wanting you home and I'm longing to see you again already, dear.

They didn't know that this was to be the last time they would see each other for five and a half months. Jack continued:

Have been flying today and we are on 'ops' tonight. The weather is terrible again, very windy and rainy, but no mist – yet . . . We must hope that the next few days will pass quickly and that we shall be together very soon . . .

At the same time Mary was writing:

I hope you will be alright on 'ops' sweet, *please* look after yourself, cos I couldn't bear anything to happen now, as we are so happy together, and I'm sure we are an 'ideal couple' . . . I just can't tell you how much I enjoyed my short stay with you. It was heaven in spite of the 'ops' on Saturday, but we sure made up for that on Sunday morning . . . I hope there's no 'ops' tonight. I'll keep my fingers crossed for you, so keep smiling, and love me lots, always . . . See you soon dearest, and once more thanks for a really grand time. You don't know how happy I am and how much married life means to me with the only fellow who I could ever love . . .

Jack never read this letter and it was returned to sender on the night of Tuesday 5 August 1941. Jack Newton's aircraft was forced to make a crash landing in Antwerp, in occupied Belgium.

On 6 August 1941, Mary received a telegram:

Regret to inform you that your husband Sgt. J. Lamport Newton is missing as result of air operations, 6/8/41 stop Letter follows stop any further information received will be immediately communicated to you.

THE FIRST LETTER AFTER OUR MARRIAGE.

THE LAST LETTER BEFORE YOU WERE MISSING.

and on the 9th,

I regret to confirm that your husband . . . is missing, the aircraft of
which he was an air gunner having failed to return to its base on
6th August 1941 after an operational flight. This does not necess-
arily mean that he is killed or wounded. I will communicate with
you again immediately if I have further news and would be obliged
if you, on your part, would write to me should you hear anything
of your husband from unofficial sources.

May I assure you of the sympathy of the Royal Air Force with
you in your anxiety . . .

Mary was devastated, but 'refused to believe he was dead . . . I kept
waiting and received tremendous support from my friends and family. I
always had a feeling that he was all right . . . he always had a lucky
streak.'

On 26 September, Mary started 'My Diary for you' in which she
wrote to Jack every day.

I would have started this diary to you sooner, darling, but I just
couldn't take any interest in things for a while, so please forgive
sweet and I'll start now.

The first entry reads:

I lay thinking about you sweetheart wondering where you are, and
how you must be worrying about me. Goodnight dearest and God
bless you and bring you safely back to me . . .

'I didn't become religious but had a gut feeling that Jack would be
all right.'

On 27 September, she wrote,

Hallo, Sweet Good Morning!! our love for each other seems so different from other peoples, that's why I'm so convinced that God will bring you back, for I am lost without you.

She missed his letters and 'kind little ways'.

The entry for 8 October 1941 mentioned that the Red Cross, whom Mary had contacted, had given her address to the sister of another crew member, a Mrs Brewer. Mrs Brewer had just written to Mary with the news that two of the crew had been taken POW; names were not given. This gave Mary hope. 'What was now important was that some news had come through. There was now hope. If two were alive, maybe others were too . . .'

On 9 October,

The air ministry confirm that one is a P.O.W. . . . it can't be you because next of kin are always informed. However I feel happier now, as your plane must have come down on land and I know what a little daredevil you are. You'll be lucky and get home somehow to me . . .

In order to 'stop myself from going crazy', Mary went almost daily to the cinema. She 'couldn't be alone in the flat because of thinking about you too much'.

By 3 November, the air ministry confirmed that two members of the crew were POWs and that nothing had been heard about the others.

I bet you're all hiding somewhere. Oh I do hope so.

Three days later, Mary felt 'years younger'. She had heard that

other crew members were safe and well and are in good hands and not prisoners. I knew it I knew it, you'll be walking in before Xmas. What a difference in me now. I pray we'll be reunited soon.

Mary was given the address of the next of kin of the other crew members and made contact with them. One by one, she heard from them. By 17 November, four crew members had been accounted for; Jack was not among them.

I am still worrying and wondering where you are.

The next day another letter arrived confirming that a fifth crew member had been taken prisoner.

I wonder if you are still at large. I mustn't give up hope though, that would never do . . .

Although the waiting was awful for Mary, she was aware that it could have been worse and that, like many others, she could have lost her husband. On 22 December, she heard indirectly that Jack was OK. The news was old and inaccurate.

Just as she was beginning to despair, she had a visit, on the evening of 30 December, from

an extremely nice gentleman, who told me he had been with you since August 6th. He is a Belgian and I just sat there in a daze, I just can't realise that you are alive and well.

This was the first piece of concrete news that Mary had received in five months. A week later on 7 January 1942:

Today has been the grandest day of my life. I've had a cable from YOU. I couldn't help crying. You are 'safe' at Gibraltar. I'm just counting the hours . . . I'm longing for our reunion.

The last entry in Mary's diary is dated 13 January 1942:

sent you a cable today dear ... nothing else of importance has happened.

That night Jack Newton arrived back in Wales. He was reunited with Mary two days later.

The aircraft in which Jack had been flying was shot down during the bank holiday raid on 5 August 1941. It landed on a German-occupied airstrip near Antwerp. The crew all escaped into the countryside. Jack was found two days after the crash by a member of the Belgian resistance movement. The leader of this escape line was a twenty-year-old girl called Dedee. She took Jack and two other airmen right across France on public transport to the Spanish border, via Paris, dressed as French peasants. There they met a Spanish Basque guide who took them across the Pyrenees on foot to San Sebastien. They went on to the British Embassy in Madrid and then on to Gibraltar.

Jack was the first British airman to be helped on the escape line Cometé. He returned home via a Sunderland flying boat. On his return he was given £1, a transit note and a cheese sandwich, and told to make his way to London, to be interrogated. Two days later, he was allowed to be reunited with his wife.

'The telegram Jack sent me from Gibraltar was the first proof I had that he was alive and I shall treasure it for always because I knew I had a future to look forward to ... that telegram changed my life ... We have been married now for fifty-three years, have three children and ten grandchildren and consider ourselves very lucky we have all these assets.'

It was also his last letter home.

DAF1078 TWICKENHAM 32/31 7
ELT 742570 SGT JACK L NEWTON C/O BRITISH CONSUL GIBRALTAR –
DARLING RECEIVED CABLE OVER JOYED YOU ARE SAFE LONGING FOR OUR REUNION TAKE CARE OF YOURSELF TONS OF LOVE

MARY NEWTON

JOAN &
PETER JACKSON

Joan Tamlin first met Peter Jackson when they were next-door neighbours as children. She was fourteen, he was fifteen. Her family had moved next door to his in Shirley, and they became friends despite Joan's mother's disapproval. Peter became an electrical engineer in a factory when he left school, and the very fact that he wore overalls to work was enough for Joan's mother. 'Also she was anti-men, my mother, I'm sure that's why I suppressed my feelings for Peter to begin with.'

When he joined the Territorial Army in 1939 with his pals from GEC, where he worked, he was called up almost immediately and was sent to France in 1939. They wrote from the time he was called up: as neighbours in 1939, as young lovers in 1944, as a married couple in 1945, and demobbed in 1946; seven years of letters.

'At the beginning I was only interested in him as a friend: I was uninterested as far as love was concerned. I was even engaged to another man, Leslie, in 1940. Mind you, I think I loved the uniform and not the man; he had a red tunic and navy trousers: he looked very glamorous.'

Joan recollects that it must have been awful for Peter that she confided so much in him, especially about Leslie and the engagement. 'Peter was the first to know in 1940 that it was on, and in 1941, that it was off . . .' He was a very close friend. Later on 11 November 1944, Peter was to write that she was 'ungettable at, as if [there was] a barrier between us'. But for now, as Joan recalls: 'I grizzled about Leslie to Peter and only then began to realize, I suppose, my fondness for him. It dawned on me I couldn't do without him. He was my right arm. He had always just been there and now I wanted him to be there. It all started in the letters . . . falling in love, I mean. It was gradual . . . the earth didn't move. I just couldn't do without him.'

From 1939 to 1941, the letters were friendly, no more. Between 1941 and 1943, Peter was in the Middle East, Sicily and Italy. During the Africa campaign, after the engagement with Leslie was broken, Joan's letters became more intimate, and when the Desert Rats of the Eighth Army came back to England to re-train (for France and to 'finish Hitler off'), Peter and Joan saw each other in a new light. Joan recalls their first meeting since she 'changed for him . . .': 'I felt terrible; this was the first time I was going to see him after I had declared myself. I was choking and frightened to death. I met him at the New Street Station, Birmingham. I saw him on the bridge. We looked at each other and just said

"Hello". That was it. Can you imagine? Later, Peter said to me "I hope you know which side your bread is buttered."'

On 24 February 1944, while on leave from the re-training camp in Sussex, Peter and Joan got engaged. Soon after, he went to France. He was away until January 1946.

The letters that Joan has kept start from June 1944. They express extreme emotion on three counts: his love for Joan, his hatred of their separation and his impatience to get back to Civvy Street. It was this that kept him alive until his demobilization in February 1946.

On 5 July 1944 he wrote:

My idea of heaven on this earth is to be as near as possible to you for the rest of my life. I couldn't possibly ask for anything more wonderful, if it wasn't for you darling, I don't think I'd really care if I died tomorrow. I'm just living for the day when I can hold you in my arms forever . . . It's not a dream, is it darling? . . . It's a heart aching experience, loving you like I do and being away from you. I love you from the bottom of my heart. I can't say more than that.

and on 5 November,

It's useless for me to attempt to put it [love] into words. You'll have to wait until you see me and then you'll see it in my eyes and I in yours . . . how lovely it would be to have you cuddling at the side of me . . .

Their limited physical contact during the February 1944 leave had 'carried him away', and Peter felt that in the army 'one's morals are apt to get corrupted or put politely, broadened . . .' He did not want to break that 'code of morals' although it was hard to live up to.

On 17 January 1945, Peter had leave for a week. He wrote on his return:

We should congratulate ourselves for controlling ourselves as well as we did . . . That's why I was so tired . . . I don't think I've ever felt so tired before . . .

This separation was hard for him and from then on he seemed very unsettled:

Darling, I never realised until now that love could be so cruel. It hurts terribly especially when I think of all those moments we had together. If being married is only half as wonderful and I know it will be twice as wonderful, then I wish I could have been married a hundred years ago. I've never prayed so hard in my life for the war to end and for my next leave, as I am now . . .

The enforced separation and his adoration made him panic and feel very anxious about the wedding; Joan was organizing it, the ring, the outfit, Peter's speech and the honeymoon. Peter was worried about . . .

what to do with my hat . . . you certainly seem between you to have pushed on with the arrangements . . . You want me to get married in my uniform . . . I haven't much choice in the matter . . . I've forgotten one thing – the honeymoon . . . if we go to Broadway, where do we stay?

On 17 April he says that his next leave is in July; their wedding time. From this point, he gets more anxious at the impending marriage, asks her to make decisions, wonders who will be the shyest on their wedding night.

Darling, have you ever realised how much it means to a man to have someone like you who can face the world unashamed in white. Darling, I think it's the most priceless possession a girl can have and I am more glad than ever that we did nothing to spoil it, however great the temptation on my last leave . . .

As his leave approached, Peter got more despondent about the world around him. He was in Germany on VE Day; his unit was fed up because they wanted to be home: 'The high ranking officers got drunk; we got a double issue of rum.' Some of his colleagues found some wood alcohol; they got very drunk and very sick. The outcome was six men dead and one blinded. Peter was upset with how unfair life was and Joan felt the same: 'The war wasn't over for me. VE Day wasn't a fabulous celebration, because my man was still in uniform. The peace was very fragile. I was working in Solihull; I would cycle to work to take my mind off it. At night in my room, it would hit me. It was a pretty fractious time.'

A month later Peter wrote:

Thank goodness I'll soon be out of the army for good. Civilian life seems like a Utopia compared to this.

Unsure about the morality of war, unsure about his ability to write letters, to make decisions, where to go on honeymoon, Birkenhead or Broadway, he announced he would arrive home three days before the wedding, set for 28 July 1945.

The honeymoon was a bit of a disaster: they had single beds and Joan got bronchitis. 'Although I wanted Peter back for good, I didn't look forward to his return because we were staying with my parents. I dreaded it . . . It was the most appalling time in my whole life.'

Peter's letters after the wedding are equally depressed. He was 'lost' without Joan and frustrated that the war had not ended for him. On 17 October he wrote to her:

This waiting, waiting, waiting all the time. I keep wondering how much longer I can stand it . . . I didn't know it could be so painful. I sometimes fear that something might take you away from me.

According to Joan, 'he was a very demonstrative person. Out of doors, though, he wasn't. He would never hold hands in public, he would shake them off.' So when he wrote on 26 January 1946:

I won't let you know when I'm coming. You'll just find me on the doorstep. I can almost see it now. I hope I shant be too much of a shock. It's the last shock of that sort you're going to get from me anyway . . .

Joan knew what he was getting at. He wanted to hug her privately.

The last letter Peter wrote to Joan was on 20 February 1946. It is self-explanatory.

> L/CPL F. D. Jackson 7607914
> 4th Armed Bde W/S
> R.E.M.E.BAOR.
>
> Feb 20th

My Darling Joan

This is, I hope, the last letter that I'll write as a civilian in Battle-Dress. If there are no unexpected delays I should be with you to stay on Monday evening. For six long years I've been waiting for the day that I could write this last letter to you.

We are about to start our married life together in earnest, & I pray that we'll make a success of it. At times it won't be easy. There will be a lot of hard work, but also an untold wealth of happiness ahead. As you know one rarely gets something for nothing in this world, either in marriage or any other sphere. However we have everything in our favour for our future success. We have a complete love & trust in each other, & similar ideals in the important things of life.

When I read & think of all the marriages that end on the rocks, I wonder if these people were ever in love like we are. Could they ever have experienced that aching loneliness, that half life that we have led these weary months? I think not.

This separation has shown me, perhaps more than anything, how much you mean to me. I've sat here many a night & wondered how I'd manage to drag through the next few weeks. They seemed an entirety. I've touched the very depths of misery, & reached the heights of ecstasy since our marriage. I've only just begun to live. I pray that I'll always be able to hold you in my arms and tell you how much I love you & to know that you love me too. Oh! My Darling what more could any man wish for. I have all the riches of Heaven & Earth in you Dearest. Dearest One I love you from the very depth of my being

Always & for ever
Yours to have & to hold

Peter

xxxxxxx

xxxxxxx

xxxxxxx

X

Peter and Joan were married for thirty-nine years, and had two children. They moved to Shropshire in 1969 to run a shop, which, as country lovers who enjoyed walking the hills and gardening, suited them perfectly. Joan says, 'I was the stronger character, he relied on me. Peter never asserted himself, but he wasn't a weak man. I only ever remember him losing his temper twice. When Peter died I started to read all the letters again, but I had to stop it, it upset me too much. I burnt some of them, even the very affectionate ones. I feel he has never left me. I still talk to him, and rarely go out in the car without asking him if he's coming with me. Very recently I started to read the letters again. He should be here still. I feel, in a curious way, that he still is. I could never marry anyone else again. From the moment our letters became romantic, we both knew it was just right.'

MARIE &
RON COX

Marie first met Ron – Percy Ronald Cox – on holiday with her parents in 1937. They were both twenty, Marie six months to the day older. She was born on 12 December, he the following 12 June.

'My father thought he was a nice young man and invited him to join us on some trips in our car. We went out on our own a couple of times, and to church together on the Sunday morning, but we lived two hundred miles apart, and it was too far away for us to meet. He asked for my home address, and would write occasionally, or send a card when he was on holiday.

'Two years later, in 1939, Ron sent a card from the Isle of Wight saying that he had to leave immediately and miss a week's holiday, and my father read it – all our mail was put on the mantelpiece – and thought what a shame. He knew what it was like, he'd been in the Navy in World War I, and felt sorry for Ron, and suggested he could spend his holiday week with us. I wrote back, and Ron came and spent a week with us, we'd already got two evacuees staying with us, but my parents didn't mind. He said he'd love to come back at Christmas, although he had to have Christmas dinner with his family. It was a very happy meeting, but at that stage there was no engagement, he had girlfriends in Bristol and I had boys from the village and from school. Ron was hoping to go into the Navy. As young as I was, if he'd said that Christmas, what about getting engaged, I possibly would have said "Yes". There was a certain feeling between us, and on our walks together that first time on holiday I'd felt it, and thought what a pity he lives so far away. I wouldn't have suggested anything, girls always waited to be invited then, it was thought very wrong to be forward.'

In 1940, still writing to each other, albeit infrequently, Marie received a letter from Ron saying that he'd just got engaged to someone else. 'I wasn't too surprised, we lived so far apart. I was very keen on him, but life had begun to be very uncertain, and I understood.'

A year later, Marie received a letter from Ron's mother, who knew of their friendship, telling her that he had gone missing in the battle of Crete, and that his engagement had been broken off. Although Marie and Mrs Cox hadn't met, Marie immediately wrote back saying how sorry she was.

Ron's mother wrote again, once she had found out that he had been sent to a prisoner-of-war camp in Germany after being taken prisoner in May 1941. He had been badly wounded and had spent time in a field hospital on Crete before being sent to the camp. He was lucky to be alive.

Marie soon started writing to Ron again. As their relationship grew through their correspondence, Marie grew certain from Ron's letters that he was hoping to come home and marry her. Meanwhile, Marie, who had volunteered for the WAAF in November 1941, did what should have been six months' radio training in two, and was sent to West Malting in Kent for fifteen months. She was then sent to Lincolnshire, Yorkshire and lastly to the Pathfinder Station at RAF Oakington in Cambridge.

'During the four years I was in the service, despite all the opportunities, I didn't make any dates, not individually anyway, going out with a group of friends was different. One day, it must have been in about January 1945, I was sitting in the hut waiting before going on duty at midnight when one of the girls came in and said there was going to be a wonderful dance at the camp that night. It was a lovely evening, with really good music. One of the pilots asked me if I'd like to dance. I was in flying control speaking directly to the pilots so I said, "Yes." He asked me to have dinner with him in Cambridge. I said that I was engaged, but he persuaded me that it wouldn't hurt, and when he rang me I went. Two or three days later when I was in flying control the news came through that he'd gone down, his was the last Lancaster of Seven Squadron to go. We couldn't dwell on things, those were the days when you could be on duty the next night and a girl would turn to you and say her brother had just gone. Every day was like that. It was the same for my brother in the RAF in the battle of Britain, nobody knew what was happening to anybody.'

Then, towards the end of 1944, the letters from Ron stopped. He was in a POW camp on the Polish border, but they were on the march to avoid being caught in the cross-fire between the advancing Allied troops and the Germans. 'I was terribly worried. I had heard rumours that they were on the march, and that one section had been strafed by planes. I really didn't know if he was alive or dead.'

Four months later, a letter at last arrived and, luckily, Marie was at home on weekend leave to receive it:

My Dear Marie,

That long awaited day, has at last arrived, as the Americans secured our release, a week ago, and at long last my freedom has been obtained. This no doubt will be the first letter you have had from me for ages, as the greater part of this year has been spent in travelling around Germany, firstly to escape the 'Bolshevic Terror', secondly to escape 'the American Gangsters' who finally caught up with us. Despite everything, I am fit and well and just waiting at a minutes notice to be taken by air to dear old England. I don't quite know how long before I am actually home, but at the first opportunity I shall wire you, and let you know exactly what is happening.

Well, Marie, it has been a long and tedious wait for both of us, and I think we shall both be rewarded, by a life-long happiness, what more can we ask. All our dreams of the future, which at one time seemed so remote, are now about to be realized, just as we wish them to be. I am afraid, this is all very rambling but, it is such a difficult letter to write, such a lot to say, but don't know how to say it. See you soon.

Yours with all my love,
Ron

'I was terribly excited, and went hastening back to camp to the WAAF officer to ask for leave, which I got. Ron sent a wire to say he was arriving on Cambridge station at 10 a.m. on 17 May. He'd never seen me in uniform, and I hadn't seen him for almost five and a half years. I can remember him saying, "What are we going to do now?", to which I replied, "Let's have a cup of tea." So that's what we did on Cambridge station. We had arranged to go away together. I had got a week's leave, but I remember saying we ought to go home to my parents first to get my civilian clothes. My parents were very pleased and excited for me. We spent the night at their house and then caught the train to London and then to the coast at Southsea, where we found a guest house. He didn't know anything about spending money or transport, he had been locked away for four years. He bought me a silver cross on a chain in Southsea.

'On 19 January 1946 we finally got married at Little Clacton where I'd been brought up. When my mother first set eyes on him again when he returned, she said, "My goodness, he'll certainly need some feeding up."

'It took him some years to get back his confidence. He was a very soft, very caring man. Killing humans wasn't his game at all.

'When I'd seen the planes go off with the bombs on board and the men not coming back, I'd thought they're doing that to bring him back to me. You had to rationalize it – all those boys were lost helping to finish the war, and my boy came home. But you felt so awful for them. It's no wonder something like that sticks with you. We were lucky, we had a wonderful reunion. As the years went by he said, "We should have been married earlier." We were married for thirty-eight years, he died in February 1984. At least we had those years together. I've never, ever wanted anybody else, I could never envisage getting married again. Not for me. I could never picture anyone else living with me in the same way, it's against my ideals.'

This last letter is the only one Marie has kept, she destroyed all the others because she didn't want anyone else to read them, they were too personal, too romantic. 'I read it a lot. I read it sometimes before I go to bed at night. I keep it inside the Bible that was given to Ron in 1929, which I keep next to my bed. I am a very sentimental person. When I read it, I always think what deep feelings he must have had to have been able to write such a letter.'

STAN &
EVA TILBURY

Stan and Eva Tilbury got married on 28 March 1932, and have been happily together for sixty-three years. Stan, at eighty-five, is six years older than his wife. They met when Eva was fifteen, at a football match in which Stan was playing. Eva had gone along with her girlfriend to watch, and at half-time Stan came over and spoke to them and asked Eva if he could take her out. Was it love at first sight?

Stan: 'I can't remember!'
Eva: 'It was for me.'
Stan: 'I stood her up on the first date. I was late back for it and she'd gone. I bumped into her and her friend by chance at ten o'clock that night – I should've met her at seven.'
Eva: 'He made an excuse and I believed him. I had fallen for him. My friend had said, "Never mind, we'll find someone else," when he hadn't turned up. Anyway he talked me round.'

They courted for nearly two years before they were married. They had never been apart before the war and were certainly not prepared for nearly four and a half years' separation.

Stan was called up in 1941, when he was thirty, and sailed that March. All he knew was that he must be going somewhere hot because of the tropical kit with which he was issued. He was a batman in the 8th Army and was sent out to the Middle East. Initially he was in Egypt, then went to Syria and Palestine before coming back to Egypt. Being continuously on the move, and in the desert, meant that it often took a long time for letters to catch up with him. When he left for the war, he and Eva had a five-year-old daughter, Daphne.

They had never written to each other before then because they had never been apart. For the first six months Eva was at home with Daphne waiting increasingly anxiously for news that Stan was all right. She wrote in desperation to the War Office and to her MP asking them, but received no reply. She became more agitated: 'I was terrible. I was under the doctor all the time there was no news. I suffered from depression, my nerves were so bad I was on pills, and the doctor finally sent me to a specialist as I didn't get any better. The specialist asked me if I was going to commit suicide. It was the no news that got me down. The moment I started getting Stan's letters I was all right, and it brought us closer together. He wanted me to tell him how Daphne was getting on, but most of all he wanted photographs. He said in his letters that it was only my letters that kept him going. "Thank God my letters came through today," he used to say.'

Stan obviously longed for the day he would never have to write another letter. In one he wrote: 'I shall be glad when I can throw this pen away too. Don't you ever ask me to write any letters when I come home dear it might start another war if you do. I often think of how many I wrote before it started. That's made you smile I'll bet.'

Eva lived in hope that his letters would be long and substantial: 'I was trembling when the post came, and even if I got a letter, if it was short I was disappointed. Stan wasn't much of a writer at first, but he got nice and sloppy by the end.'

13082470 Pte Tilbury S.
38 Salvage Unit
M.E.F.

March 28

My Darling,

How are you feeling today? I never thought that we would ever be parted for our ninth and tenth anniversaries. I think of you darling more as time goes on. How glad I shall be when we are together again for good. I miss you very much darling, more than words can explain. One consolation I get is when I open my wallet and see your photo which I always carry with me. It made me very proud last night when Sandy called my number out and I received your message. The first one in our unit to come over the air. Just think of it dear all the lads in the unit waiting for messages every Friday and ours the first. You ought to have heard the cheer go up when we heard it. I bet Daphne was excited when she heard her name mentioned. By the time this reaches you sweetheart I don't think that we shall be in the desert as we are going to Syria. Whatever it's like out there it can't be worse than here. Don't worry darling I shall be O.K. I am sending a few more photos. Hope you have received the others. Sorry this is only a short letter dearest but I am rather busy and have to get a bath sometime this afternoon. Roll on the time when this is all over and we three are happy at home again. Darling I'll love you always, so look after yourself til I return.

Time is getting on so I'll have to close now. Goodbye for the present sweetheart, my love is all yours,

Stan

'Sandy' is Sandy MacPherson who presented *Forces Calling* from the Blackpool Tower. Eva had sent in a request for their favourite record – 'If I Had A Talking Picture Of You' – to be played on their wedding anniversary on 28 March.

Stan remembers the shock and surprise he felt: 'There were just over a dozen in our unit in the tent. I'd just taken the battery off the motor and fixed it in so we could hear the wireless. I was somewhere in the desert behind enemy lines. As the wireless came on, our request was the first thing I heard, the record that Eva had requested for me. At the end, such a big cheer went up in the tent I couldn't hear what he said, but I remember one bloke shouting out, "Who on earth would want a talking picture of you?"'

Talking or otherwise, pictures were a vital way of keeping in touch, as Eva recalls: 'Photographs became as important a diary of events as letters. Stan would say, "For God's sake keep the photos coming", so I kept on having them taken whenever I could afford to. It was a job to get film.'

When Eva finally heard Stan was on his way home she set to work on

Prefix. Time handed in. Office of Origin and Service Instructions. Words.

98

From   98 9.15 SOUTHAMPTON 14   To

MRS TILBURY 15 KINGSHILL RD TERRIERS HIGHWYCOMBE BUCKS

5 = ARRIVED SOUTHAMPTON EXPECT HOME SHORTLY   = STAN

+ 15 +

his birthday/homecoming cake. She had saved all her rations to make his favourite fruitcake. She had bought a chicken shed and four chickens with £3 Stan had sent her, so she even had fresh eggs.

Daphne was the first to see her father coming in through the kitchen door. Eva was in the larder with the plates. Daphne remembers hearing her mother banging the plates down, and not knowing whether they were broken. Then her father turned to her and said he'd got something in his bag for her: 'To get me out of the way I think.'

Eva: 'Well what do you expect after four years!'

Daphne and Eva nearly went mad with excitement. Everyone hugged each other and they cut the homecoming cake. Then Stan and Eva settled down to married life again. They soon had another daughter, Linda, who was born in 1946. Their son David was born in 1950. Eva has kept all Stan's letters. They are in a plastic bag at the back of her wardrobe. If ever she's feeling a bit down she gets them out and reads them. 'We haven't been apart since the war. It was too damn long, and we haven't made up for it yet, have we?!'

ALBERT
RICHARDSON

Just before he sailed to North Africa in 1942, Albert Richardson wrote a last, hasty letter to his wife Grace and daughter Pat. Barely more than a scrawled note, it still manages to convey optimism, love and an entreaty to his wife to stay faithful in his absence. It was written on 9 December, and marked the beginning of a correspondence that was to last through all the years of separation, not ending until the spring of 1945.

Tues 4 pm

Darling sweetheart Grace and Pat,

Just a short letter to you. If you have not sent that piece of paper Please don't send it. Our letters are all censored from tonight when we move off to a port. Don't worry sweetheart I will love you for ever and ever also our Sal and I WILL RETURN TO YOU AGAIN. I will write to you as often as possible. Look after yourself – so I still have you when I return which won't be long I'm sure. Do be a good wife while I'm away sweetheart. I shall go knowing that you love me, and look after our Sal for me. Darling I WILL write again later to you.

God Bless you Both

Love from Your Dearest Husband,
Albert XXXX
XXXXX

Within months Albert was taken prisoner in the Kasserine Pass and was shipped to Germany. Like so many others, he lived for his letters, and dreamed of the future. He looked forward to freedom, to roaming the fields, to having an allotment, but most of all to returning to his wife and daughter. 'DON'T WORRY. I have planned a happy life for us after all this.'

Pat, then aged seven, wrote to him in the camp:

Dear Daddy,

I hope you are still alright. Mam and me fetched the fishes in the other day. I hope it wont be long before you are home again with Mam and me to keep you company. We went to the pictures last night to see, my gal Sal. We wished that you could have been there too. I think that is all for now. Bye-Bye Love from your old gal Sal.

XXXXXXXXXXXXXXXX

Dear Daddy

I hope you are alright and I hope you got my last letter. Mam has had some letters from you and thank you for your letter to me. I have got a real school girls hat made of felt with a rim that turns up. I hope it won't be long before you are home again with mam and me.

Bye-Bye, Love from
     Love Pat
xxxxxxxxxxxxxxxxxxxxxxx
xxxxxxxxxxxxxxxxxxxxxxx
xxxxxxxxxxxxxxxxxxxxxxx
xxxxxxxxxxxxxxxxxxxxxxx
xxxxxxxxxxxxxxxxxxxxxxx

In February 1945, as the end of the war drew near, Albert wrote anticipating his return and his first sight of the English shore, Dover's white cliffs, and home:

18th February 1945

Dear Grace and Pat,

Keep Smiling.

Still keeping well in every way I wonder if this letter will reach you as mail is very bad just now, it must be the same with you, but it is a good sign. Red X parcels are also very scarce now, doubt if we ever see anymore of those but I am alright for food, also clothes. Just 'Roll on that Boat' I hope towards the cliffs of Dover nearly 2 years since POW on the 21 Feb. I have had quite enough of it too, you do get a bit of freedom going out to work not like Italy behind barbed wire all the while. I am waiting for those Sunday evening walks again and pictures of course, not forgetting my paradise 'The Warren' the soon the better. I have had 3 clothing parcels from you and 14 Cigs parcels amounting to 3400 Cigs, and 12 two oz tins of tobacco, which is very good. I had my photo taken twice with working party, don't know if ever we shall see them, hope so. I have worn that woolen helmet this winter on very cold days instead of hat quite warm too.

Hope my big Gal is alright. Tell her I won't be long now. Remember me to all friends. Just Roll on the Boat. Don't Worry Dear I alright.

Love Albert

When Albert was at last liberated by the Americans in April 1945, he was flown home from Brussels to be reunited with his wife and daughter. Within a year of arriving home, Grace and Albert had their second child, Alan, who was born in March 1946.

JOHN DOSSETT-DAVIES & ELLEN MONNICH

John Dossett-Davies joined the army in the spring of 1945, and was posted to Trieste in northern Italy. He had been on draft to go to the Far East, but was diverted after Hiroshima. He was in Trieste for almost three years, until his demobilization in July 1948.

He has vivid memories of journeying through Germany after its collapse. '. . . the journeys up from Italy through the shattered cities of the Ruhr, with buildings, like skeletons, just the outside walls standing, still made a great impression on me. My train trundled slowly through the empty, silent ruins of Essen. The massive destruction, the poverty of the German people and the harsh winter that year contrasted with the sunshine of the south. There were sixty million refugees and displaced persons moving around, or in camps, waiting to be repatriated or resettled in other continents. The Ruhr was a mass of rubble and people lived in cellars or in holes in the ground. Although it may sound strange, despite all the damage and the post-war problems, it was a marvellous time to be young in Europe, immediately after the war. There was a special feeling in the air that the continent was being born again.'

It was on a trip to Gottingen to study at the College of the Rhine Army that he first fell in love. He was twenty. He met Ellen Monnich through an Army colleague who was friendly with her sister. At weekends, and whenever John had an evening off, they would meet by Schiller's statue. He nicknamed her Dizzy, she nicknamed him Jack. She was twenty-two, eighteen months older than John, a small, fair-haired girl with quite a good command of English, and a lovely singing voice. She would sing German songs to John, like 'Der Liebe Augustine'. Together they went to Hamelin in Brunswick, where the Pied Piper led first the rats and then the children away, and she told him stories from the Brothers Grimm who had been librarians in Gottingen.

'Our love affair, in fact, was quite idyllic, like a fairy story set in a fairy tale land.' Gottingen was, and still is, a romantically beautiful old medieval town, with most of its ancient ramparts still intact. John's initial trip to Gottingen lasted only about eight weeks; he then went back to Italy. They met as often as they could, going for walks in the woods just outside the town, to the cinema, and visiting Dizzy's home and her relatives. At night they would look up at the stars and give each other a star from Orion's belt to look at when they were apart. Each would look

at the star at an agreed time, knowing the other was thinking of them and doing the same many miles away.

They talked a lot about politics. Having seen Europe so devastated, John felt any price was worth paying rather than going through that again. 'So my love affair was very important in that respect.' Ellen's parents were not opposed to the relationship. 'The English were looked on as quite affluent, and there were no young German men around, they were either dead, limbless or prisoners of war. Germany was bereft of young men. Gottingen was very near the border, so the Germans were frightened of Russia.'

John got to know Ellen's family quite well. He took them food to keep them going at a difficult time when Germany was in a very poor way. He even thought of smuggling Ellen into his camp for a meal when she was hungry, but could not find a uniform small enough for her. He gave the family a US Army blanket and they made it into an elegant dress. 'I remember her mother made the most excruciating coffee – quite undrinkable – which I managed to get down. It was, I believe, made from acorns. Ellen made me a cake for my twenty-first birthday, and gave me a briefcase and an engraved silver ring. I sent her a handbag and some elegant shoes from Italy after she sent me a size pattern of her feet.'

Ellen's letters included leaves and bits of twigs from the tree they sat under together, and told of her determination to stay faithful to John and await his return. 'Her letters traced the poignant path of our love affair.'

Gottingen, 16th of April, 1948

My Dear Jack,

Now I am alone again the second time. Never before it was so heavy for me to say 'good by'. It will be take a long time till I see you again but I shall wait. Because I know you love me and you think of me always.

I shall be very happy when I shall get a letter from you. Don't forget to look to the stars in the night. They bring the kind regards to you from me. Do you remember what we said about this? I do it and all my love and thoughts are with you dearest.

Well, dear, thanks again for the lovely time I spent with you,

for all that you did do for me. I never stop to love you. Don't forget
that I wait for you as long as you like.

Now you are away and I have only my work. I thank you again
for your last present you give to me. I like everything you give to
me. Well, dear, was it heavy for you, too, to say 'good by'? Inside
me everything was dark because you were away. Why we must part
again? But I don't want to make your heart heavy and so I wait till
you come.

I close now and I give all my love to you.

Your Dizzy.

xxxxxxxxxxxxxxx

Gottingen

My Dear Jack,

Many thanks for your welcomed letter dated from the 4th of June.
I am so terrible sorry you had had no letter from me for 3 weeks.
And so had not I. I thought many silly things what might be
happened with you or you don't love me no more. I beg your
pardon but I miss your letter so very much.

And then came your letter and made me very happy. I am not
interested in the soldiers who are coming and going, I only love
you so much, that it does hurt me. And don't forget what I
promised you in our last night. My love is great enough to stay
against everything.

Well, dearest, I have hoped you would come once more on a
course to Gottingen, but you did not. I always think of you and
write to you but it's not my fault that you did not get my letter it
must be something wrong with the post. Every time I get a letter
from you, I look forward to your next one.

We have marvellous weather. Every day sunshine and blue
skies. Every night before I go to our garden, I go swim. Some
nights I go in our park and sit on our place and dream of you.
These are the best hours of the day for me. Your big photo is
hanging in our sitting-room above that chair you sat on when you
were in our house. So I see you always when I work, eat and do

nothing and I feel you close to me. By the way have you send the shoes to me? I didn't get anything and so I hope it does not get lost. But I am sorry if I have remind you, I did not want to do that. My sister is in your home now. She left Gottingen on the 24th May and she likes it very much over there. She knows many English people and they are all very kind to her. When will I see my sister over there? That will take a longtime, I suppose.

Is your mother in London now and how she is getting on? If it is come true what we thought, I shall have only 40 minutes by train to come to her. I mean my sister.

But I close now and send all my love to you. Never think I will be unfaithfull to you, you are my love, longing and my world. I only live in you and long to be only you for always and always.

Your Dizzy

On his return home in 1948, John had been certain of one thing, his love for Ellen. 'When I left her I fully intended, in due course, to send for her and marry her.' He had not begun to anticipate or realize the strength of anti-German feeling in England at the end of the war. He had mentioned Ellen to his family, but not that he planned to bring her home.

'I think the moment I realized it was over was when a cousin of mine, Major Jack Hamp of the Royal Artillery, told me of his friend who wanted to marry a German girl. "One of the enemy", he called her. "I'll never speak to him again," he said. I didn't tell him of my relationship, but I felt I couldn't go on with it.'

John admits to feeling shocked by this response. He was only twenty-one when he came out of the Army, not ready for marriage, but he still feels a sense of shame at the last letter he wrote to Ellen breaking off their relationship. He didn't want to subject Ellen to the hostility that existed here in Britain, and although looking back he is aware that it didn't last long, and a lot of marriages between the Germans and the British were extremely successful, feels that at the time it was impossible to anticipate how quickly the anti-German feeling would subside.

His last letter to her is one he will never forget writing. Up until then, as with so many people during the war, their letters had been a way of talking to each other. 'Letters were like conversations. I remember sitting down to write it in the bedroom. I had thought a lot about it and delayed. I drafted it out. There was a certain amount of pretentious stuff in it like "I'm doing it for you", which wasn't true. I tried to convey I was doing it for her sake, but I should have been honest, said the truthful thing, that I was breaking it off because of the anti-German feeling. It was insulting to her that I didn't, that I made out it was a personal thing. If a letter is very important I never send it on the same day as I write it, which is what I did with Ellen's. I posted it the next morning.'

A few weeks later John received Ellen's last letter:

Gottingen 4.8.48

My Dear Jack,

Thank you for your letter which I received one hour ago. I am very sorry that you dont want write eny more to me from England. But you must now best dear, but if you sink I will ever forget you then you be rong, I love you so much and now this. I can hardly believe it. I still will wait for you if you want me too, few years would not be so much for me. If you still love me a bit, please write to me ones in two or 3 weeks only that I know how you are would be so kind. I will wait and look for word for that one letter from you. I like you so mush.

Now I think I close my letter with best wishes and all my love,

Yours Dizzy

He read it once, then put it away with all the others and some photographs in an old Army box, and didn't read them again for forty years. At the time of receiving it, he was at a very low ebb; he had left the Army and returned home to he knew not what, leaving the sunshine of Italy and friends who were still in the Forces. 'I was not sure what to do with myself. I hadn't had an education, I was lonely, and it had been so romantic in Germany. Our basic feelings had transcended everything around us. Danger is a great aphrodisiac. It's a very tender, precious memory. I don't feel entirely shamed by my last letter to her. I knew I

Guttingen 4. 8. 48.

My Dear Jack,

Thank you for your letter witch I recived one auer egau. I am very sorry that you dont wonte write eny more to me from England. But you must now hert. deer, but if you sink I will ever forget you, then you be rong. I love you so mush and now lt's I com hardly beliae it. I still will wi't for you if you wont me too, few Jährs would nat be so mush for me. If you had some living to do, some growing up to do. Half of me says I was acting responsibly, half that it was cowardly.'

In 1971, John went back to Gottingen on a trip to Germany. He returned to the house Ellen had lived in in Lenie Strasse, but the family were no longer there. Neighbours were able to tell him that Ellen had married and had a son. She had a sister in England, but when John went to see her she was not there. Since then he has happily married.

I managed to trace Ellen Monnich – now Ellen Gerlt – through an old address that John had from a public records office. One night she telephoned me. Despite her rusty English and my total lack of German, I put it to her that I would like to interview her for the film and that John had already agreed to take part. She was clearly thrilled that contact was on the point of being made again.

Everything was soon arranged and we flew to Hanover, driving from there to Gottingen. We filmed in all the places where John and Ellen had met and then went back to Ellen's flat to interview her. She was still very emotional about her relationship with John. Had his letter ending it not come, she believed they would have married. She did marry, later, but her husband had not wanted her to keep John's letters and so, regretfully, she had had to part with them. When we left, she presented me with a letter to forward to John. It had been returned to her after she had sent it. It had only the first half of his address on it.

Shortly after this, I heard that John and his wife, Anne, are planning a trip to Gottingen to see Ellen. It will be forty-seven years since their last letters to each other.

JAMES WOOZLEY
& PAM POWELL

Pam Powell was in her WAAF uniform when she met James at Cardiff station in 1939. She had got caught up with the 'great Patriotism' of the day even though she was only seventeen years old. 'We chatted and then she caught the train. I was bowled over by her – she was special.'

Six months later, by sheer coincidence, James and Pat met at a dance in Pembroke. They fell for each other. James recalls: 'We had a wonderful courting. We would go to Tenby and do a lot of walking. It was that wicked winter of 1940; there was snow in March! We did a lot of snogging in empty railway carriages.'

After nine months in Wales, James was posted to Cornwall. He was an EMT driver of service vehicles with the RAF and stayed in England until 1943. A little later, Pam went to Scotland. James received a letter from her every week for four and a half years, the length of their separation: 'The letters I received from Pam were a boost to one's morale. Receiving them made me nervous and excited. I hadn't proposed to her before we both went off because we didn't get big packets, just handouts, we decided to wait until after.'

In 1943, James was posted to Southern Rhodesia where he spent two years until he was demobbed in the autumn of 1945. Pam got very fed up and changed departments. She was posted to Cairo. 'She was moved to codes and cyphers and became an assistant section officer. She did very well, better than me.'

While in Cairo, Pam had a 'rough spell. She got seduced by and engaged to a Cairo Cavalier [Army officer]. He soon abandoned her and she went to Palestine for a spell before she ended her war at RAF Beccles in Suffolk.'

When James heard that Pam had a fiancé, he was 'devastated': 'The letter took a very long time to sink in.' But he didn't give up; James still had hopes that something would happen.

The last letter that Pam wrote to James, dated 3 October 1945, was sent to his home in Richmond, Surrey, in anticipation of his return. Pam, 'a forceful woman' was apprehensive and confused. The war had hardened her, emotionally and philosophically. Her life was in conflict.

R.A.F. Beccles
Suffolk

3/10/45

Dearest Jim,

Your last letter, which was overflowing with joie de vivre and what have you, arrived while I was on leave & I found it waiting for me when I got back. You said in it that you expected to be home in about 8 weeks, so I waited a bit before answering so that this wouldn't be too out of date, and am sending it to your home, just to say 'cheers' to you when you arrive.

You must let me know as soon as you know your movements after landing, & then we can see what is to be done about meeting; it should be possible to fix up something that is if you want to of course! But I'm warning you now that you will probably find a very different person after 4½ years – or perhaps you had realised that from letters.

Judging by the snapshot you sent, you have gone in for protective colouring – you look as black as a nigger in it – also, dare I say it, you look as though you had put on some weight! But perhaps that is just the way you are sitting or something!

Isn't it a wonderful feeling when you get back home again? The first glimpse of land as the ship comes in, & then the old familiar & newly strange sights & sounds & smells. The people & the buses & the feel of an English railway station; and above all, I think, the voices & the familiar gruff friendliness. It's all so good and so unbelievable at the same time. Honestly, it's almost worth having been abroad to come back to all that again, or so it seemed 18 months ago.

I was in London for the week-end last week, just going on a mild break-out from this god-forsaken station; and it has never looked better. Perhaps it was the sudden autumn sunshine, or perhaps because we had leisure and peace in which to look at it, or both, but it almost seemed enchanted; clean washed and clear and surprisingly beautiful – I had never really seen it before, not like that, even rural me could feel something of the essential charm of the place, so I can imagine a bit what it must be like for you, who knows it so well, to come back to it all new again.

Will you be getting your release as soon as you get home, or isn't your group up yet? They are being almighty slow with these releases blast them. Our branch of course is completely redundant now; to give us something to do we are being sent practice messages 'to keep your hand in' – what for the lord only knows. But even so, they don't set about getting rid of us, but merely push us into some other damn-fool job – so far I have escaped that, please heaven I do till the end. I'm 27 group and that means next January, at the present rate of progress – another $3\frac{1}{2}$ mortal months – and another three weeks of this damn place is going to send me raving lunatic. I have never hated any place so much in my life I think – the very name nearly makes me throw up.

By the time we meet I shall be just about mad – so if you see someone approaching in WAAF uniform and foaming at the mouth and muttering to themselves, you will know at once who it is, even without recognising me – and you quite probably won't do that by the way!

Jimmy, I don't want to seem to harp on – but I am not the same person I was you know. I think I have got harder, and I am certainly more disillusioned. There aren't many people about these days that I can put implicit faith in; some there are of course, thank heaven; but I don't expect much of people in general. I don't know how to put it, because I'm not quite certain what I want to say, but I think it's roughly this. We had a lot of fun and a very happy time at P.D. and I think we got to know each other fairly well then – in fact really well; and I for one always remember it happily; and I think you must do too, or you wouldn't have bothered to keep it up like this through so many changes and vicissitudes – and that's the danger from your point of view – don't build too much on that and expect to find it again – I'm going to be horribly frank now and probably tactless, but please try and understand – it's not going to be quite the same Jimmy, I'm not talking now about any sentiment attached but of plain fact, of our knowing each other and of being friends, the important part that has lasted out of those eight or nine months, and which has gone on through the next five years. Well, you liked me then, and I hope very much you will like me now — but you wont if you expect to find the same sort of person you knew then, because I'm not. Better or worse, or just different, I don't know, except that it is difficult. I think I know the differences there will be in you, and I also feel that whatever the surface difference may be, you will be the same old Jim underneath it all; so that it's alright from my point of view — I'm just not certain about it from yours, and I would hate for you to be disappointed in me. I seem to be taking it very much for granted that you liked the old well enough to want to find it again, aren't I? But I'm not fishing, old man, and I'm not trying to say anything and then wrapping it up. All I want to do is to tell you that I feel I am different and warn you. Gypsy's warning and all that! It's probably very self centred of me to attach so much importance to myself, with capital letters; but I do know a bit now what it is to be disappointed in anyone you like and to find a stranger where you expected a friend — and I want to spare you that — that's all, and you will probably say 'and quite enough too'. So let's leave all this, it doesn't sound awfully cheerful and welcoming does it — but it wasn't meant like that, because I am looking forward to seeing you very much indeed. Put it down to nervousness or something! After which sudden outburst of grandmotherliness we really will leave it. (But I haven't been as grandmotherly as that for a long time, have I? And I thought I was being so good these days — what a lapse!)

There really isn't much news to tell you — or if I did it wouldn't be cheerful news, because I would only bind about this place ad infinitum and ad nauseam. Anyway I'm fast becoming disgustingly self-centred, which is no way to greet the returned wanderer. It should be all trumpets and bunting, that's what you will be wanting, not to mention the real good stoop of ale. But you will be getting the welcome from your family and you will be making one for yourself by just being home; so please, I would like to add my little quota to it as well — when you get round to thinking straight again, which I imagine wont be for some time, have a pint for me. It will probably be the one you have next day to pull you round actually, as I don't imagine you will be thinking much about

There really isn't much news to tell you — or if I did it wouldn't be cheerful news, because I would only kvind about this place ad infinitum and ad nauseam. Anyway I'm fast becoming disgustingly self-centred, which is no way to greet the returned wanderer. It should be all trumpets & bunting, that's what you will be wanting, not to mention the real good sloop of ale. But you will be getting the welcome from your family & you will be making one for yourself by just being Home; so please, I would like to add my little quota to it as well — When you get round to thinking straight again, which I imagine won't be for some time, have a pint for me. It will probably be the one you have next day to pull you round actually, as I don't imagine you will be thinking much about anything before them — you will be feeling so good! Lucky devil, having a home-coming, it is so good, as I said before, it really makes everything else worth while.

This is being written in my room late in the evening over a brew of cocoa, so I raise my mug to you Timmy — Cheers and all the best — glad to see you.

Love
Pam.

P.S. I've addressed this to your Service rank etc: as I didn't know whether the Civvie form of address plus initials would get you mixed up with your father or something — which would be odd!

anything before then – you'll be feeling so good! Lucky devil, having a home-coming, it is so good as I said before, it really makes everything else worthwhile.

This is being written in my room late in the evening over a brew of cocoa, so I raise my mug to you Jimmy – Cheers – and all the best – glad to see you.

love Pam.

After his return, and having read Pam's letter, James went up to RAF Beccles to see her. 'Outwardly, she hadn't changed much. But she wasn't so approachable as before. Certainly not so affectionate. After the Cairo Cavalier she never trusted men again. She didn't like men any more and I didn't broach the subject. She had become a complete stranger, would not and did not get married and ended her days as a conservative agent in North Yorkshire.'

James did marry and had three children. He kept in touch with Pam until her death in 1992.

PART VI

VE Day

JACK & OLIVE CLARK

David Clark first remembers being aware of his parents' wartime correspondence, when, as a child, he discovered a large suitcase full of letters under the stairs. 'That was it for twenty years. When my mother, Olive, died in 1980, Dad decided whoever was left after his death should decide what to do with the letters. Dad didn't want to destroy them, so he put them in a folder engraved with the letters O and J 1942–1947. He and Mum had met in Blackburn in July 1942. Mum was twenty-six, Dad was twenty. They started writing immediately. Dad had come from Woolwich to work in the Royal Ordnance Factory, Mum was a local girl, a nurse. In 1943 his apprenticeship finished, and he was called up. He was sent all over the place, to France in June 1944, he was in Germany for VE Day, and he came home from Hong Kong in March 1947 before being demobbed in the April. Over this period they wrote nearly six hundred letters to each other, and kept them all.

'I was born in December 1944, but it was three months before Dad first saw me, and then not again for two and a half years.'

David has a clear memory of his father, a stranger, walking back into his life, and exactly what he felt about it: 'My early memories are of trying to keep him and Mum apart. I was in the bed with them, and I'd try to kick him out of it, or get angry when he told me what to do, because he was a stranger. Mum had put a picture of him by my bed when he was away, but it didn't make any difference.'

David and his sister Barbara, who was born in 1951, did not read the letters until after their father had died. Barbara describes her parents as: 'Incredibly close, a real Darby and Joan, the word devoted would not be an understatement, they went everywhere together. Dad really mourned when she died, in fact I was almost happy when he died. He was very independent, but she was his life. Reading the letters I suddenly felt I could see why, you can see how their love started, he told her everything, it's all there. They always wrote the truth, you have to mean what you write, it's a deliberate, conscious thing, you don't have to so much when you speak. They met in the July, and by the August they were in love. I know if they'd been my letters I would've burned them, but I've learned a lot about what's important in life from them. They were separated for *so* long, but it made them what they were, it helped the closeness. Every letter mentions how the separation and the letters will sustain them and keep them strong. It's just true love being expressed in words, it's like a little time capsule, that way of life and of expression has gone now. Mum's letters are so detailed, so full of mundane trivia, but *that*'s what she'd have said if he'd been there. Whether they were important or trivial snippets of life, they brought him home, brought him a sense of reality. He thought the minutiae was wonderful, it helped him focus on what he was going to return to. He always said *when* I return, not if.'

The separation that Jack felt, along with the letters, sustained him but was still something he clearly never wanted to repeat:

It's not just us being together again which I long for, but for us to be together never to be parted again which is my silent prayer.

The following three letters, written around VE Day, anticipate their renewed life together, with no further separation, which is exactly what happened on Jack's return.

41 High Street
Rishton

Sat. evening
5.5.45

My own beloved Jack,

At the long last you have ceased fighting darling and I thank God for keeping you safe for me during the last eleven months. I am now looking forward to the letters written after 8am today. Do, darling write to me as soon as you can. In the papers on Thursday it says that all BLA men are to have 28 days leave after the fighting in Germany is over so now we can look forward to the day you come home for longer than just a short seven days.

Mother and Alice were very glad when your letter came this afternoon. Alice is very happy with her work now that she has got more used to it.

We had a card from your mother this morning to say that they had now had news of Roy and that he is quite alright. It is such a long time since there was news of him and it is good to hear that so far he is O.K.

Baby's photographs have not arrived yet. I don't know when they will be ready because they are coming by post. As I have no idea how long you will have to be in Germany I am wondering what to do about sending a photograph to you. Will you let me know what you would like me to do.

Just lately I have been doing my darndest to buy a film so that we could take a snap of David. Is there any chance of you being able to buy a camera and a film for here it is just impossible to get one. There is something else I would like to ask you to get for me. Could you possibly manage to buy a bottle of perfume something like the other one you bought for me. You see I'm afraid that the other is evaporating now that it has been opened and I do like the scent of it.

For the past three days we have listened to the news every hour that we have been awake. Tonight in the last of the series 'War Review' we listened to a Dutchman describing occupied Holland during the last five years and also of the relief and happiness you have brought to their country.

My Darling I am so proud of you. So proud to know that you are my Husband and that you love me equally as much as I love you. God has blessed me in giving you for my Husband and David our son. I shall always be happy whilst you both Love me and need me.

I am just longing for you to see David again Jack. He is a real treat and no mistake. I'm sure it won't be long before he is on his hands and knees. He is always trying to get himself into some precarious position and we have to hang on to him like grim death. He is just like a jack-in-the-box.

I want to tell you Jack that we need have no anxiety now about the possibility of a forthcoming event.

Now I will go to sleep darling with loving thoughts of you dear.

Each night I think that that is one day less towards your home coming and we all hope that it will be soon.

Do hasten that lovely Day for your Loving wife and son

Olive and David

xxxxxxxxxxxxxxxxxxxxxxxxxxxxxxxxxxxxxxxxxxxxxxxxxxxxxxxxx

xxxxxxxxxxxxxxxxxxxxxxxxxxxxxxxxxxxxxxxxxxxxxxxxxxxxxxxxx

8 May 1945   2058212 Clark J
                                        B Troop 190 Bty
                                        143 Field Reg. RA
                                        B.L.A.

My Own Darling Olive,

Wasn't it wonderful news darling? In fact it seems all too good to
be true. Today – VE Day is the day we have been waiting for for as
many years but even so it doesn't seem possible somehow that we
have at last won our War. I suppose you were tremendously excited
and happy when you heard the news at home but its hard to explain
really and it may sound funny but it didn't somehow make much
impression on us when we first heard the capitulation. That was at
twenty to eight on Friday the 4th of May and only concerned our
part of the front – Holland and Northern Germany. It didn't seem
to make a lot of difference at first. We had just come in from the
O.P. and were due to go out on a practise scheme in the morning
as we were pretty browned off. It was an English speaking civilian
who came and told us and he must have thought us a pretty poor
lot because, we didn't take much notice but just went on cleaning
our Carrier! Later on in the evening we went over to the Gun
Position and did a bit of celebrating. For this purpose we dug out
our Rum Bottle and drank the contents between the four of us and
a double ration which was issued to mark the occasion as well!
Outside all around and as far as you could see the sky was full of
lights, parachute flares, and illuminating flares of all colours. There
were lines of tracer bullets and bofors shells streaming across the
sky and in fact it was a real Guy Fawkes night. That was when I
wrote that letter form to you and it is signed by our carrier crew –
the driver, the other driver op, the officer and his assistant.

    After this we had to spit and polish everything in preparation for the big march forward. Whilst we were waiting yesterday morning to move off dressed in our Sunday best with all the vehicles shining and our webbing scrubbed white we received the news from Regimental Headquarters that all resistance everywhere had ceased. This was before it was broadcast on the wireless. Our job is to go on into Holland and round up and disarm the Germans mostly S.S. troops and send them back to Germany. We started yesterday midday and came into the German lines about 25 miles. All along the roads the civilians were lined up cheering and waving flags and wearing orange shirts and ties and the girls orange dresses and ribbons and painted on the trees and walls were big slogans 'Welcome' and 'We Thank You'. We have come as far as DOORN where you remember the Kaiser was held captive since the last war. You will find this place on the map quite easily and I will be able to let you know exactly where we are in future as we have been told we can now do this. We expect to be here for about a week then are going on into Germany as Occupation troops.

It's funny here really for there are Jerries all over the place and all of them fully armed. We came into our Billet about seven o'clock yesterday evening and it was occupied by Jerries up to an hour of us arriving. Our advance party came along and told them to clear out so they just packed up and moved about 200 yards away and there they are. They ride around on bikes with rifles on their backs and some of them actually had the nerve to come and ask us for cigarettes today! You don't need a very vivid imagination to guess what our answer was. It seems so strange that everything could have altered so much in 24 hours just by the signing of a piece of paper.

On the wireless this morning we heard the official announcement of VE Day and that everyone, all over the world was celebrating it. We had no opportunity of celebrating at all and nothing to celebrate with literally not even water because the water supply has been off all day and only just come on again. Out here we always said that when Victory came the only people who would have the opportunity of celebrating would be those who did no fighting but I suppose that's just hard luck and we don't begrudge anyone who feels happy and has a good time these days.

We have a fine billet here, a large detached house in the middle
of a pine forest just outside Doorn. It's been a lovely day and
wonderfully peaceful and quiet. Now it is evening and the sun is
just going down – Darling this would be such a wonderful place to
go walking with you just you and I together with no more worries
and fears for each other.

I have your three lovely letters nos. 72, 73 and 74 which has
just arrived. Although I love reading your sweet words so much
Darling it will be wonderful when we no longer have to write
letters to each other but can speak our words of Love and Adoration
to each other.

I am on duty from midnight until four o'clock as I'm going to
bed now and will join you again in four hours time. You will be
sleeping whilst I am writing so Sleep Well Darling and God Bless
you and bring quickly the moment when we shall be lying together
in each others arms once again for I love you and long for your Love
to the very depths of my heart.

2.30

Hullo again darling. Here I am and it is very quiet and still. Except
for the sentry outside I am the only one awake in the middle of the
night. When I had finished writing last evening one of our party
produced a bottle of champagne and as well there was a rum issue
so we managed a little celebration with half a pint of Champagne
and two tots of rum each. It was a sacrilege really to drink 1934
Champagne from chipped old enamel mugs but we had no glasses
and I don't suppose it would have tasted any different if we had.

My Darling – when first I left you I said I would come back to
you again one day I meant it then and I still mean it now. The War
out here is over which of course means that there is considerably
less danger now than during the previous eleven months. However
long we shall be kept here I don't know and whether or not I shall
have to go out East or not I don't know either. But I do know my
sweetheart that the end is in sight now and it can't be very far off
before all our worries and fears are memories of the past and our
Love and Life a reality instead of a burning desire within us. It's

not just us being together again which I long for but for us to be together never to be parted again which is my silent prayer. When this occurs My Darling I want you to hold me tightly to you – to Love me and never let me go away from you again for I never want to experience again the longing for you which I have done during the last year.

Had we never met I don't know what I should have thought of Home as being. Whenever I think of Home now I vision you with your loving arms outstretched to hold me closely. David with his beautiful smile and his lovely ways, us walking hand in hand together and your Love mirrored in your eyes when we kissed in the moonlight – the tender loveliness and glorious womanhood of your beauty and the sense of completeness which only exists when we are together. If I hadn't you I wouldn't have these things to think of but you are my wife and my Darling Sweetheart and my life is built around the promise of our future together. My happiness began the moment I realised that you had Love for me and that I was acceptable to you. Oh My Darling you have always been so lovely and desirable and not only that but such a perfect and understanding companion that I should have been broken hearted had my Love and longing for you been in vain.

I am longing to see David's photograph and so hope it comes soon darling. The books still haven't arrived so I have given them up as lost by now. I feel sure you can send registered envelopes out here for we can send them back so could you see and send the other booklets out to me. I will enclose the addresses of the places I wrote to if I still have them, then if you want to you can write and get the ones which were lost.

You say thank God for the lucky star I was born under. Well I think it's just fate and that my name hasn't been on one yet. There are lots of chaps who go through a War without getting a scratch and I see no reason why I shouldn't be one of them! There are many times when I could have been killed but wasn't and someone else died instead. That's not being callous but just hard luck and something you forget as soon as possible. I'm sure that having gone as far as this and stayed in one piece I'm going to remain that way.

Our front was the first to surrender on the Western Front. You will have read in the paper that the surrender of the German 25th Army took place at Wageningen which is a town not far from Arnhem and which we liberated on the 16 April. We went in with the first tanks and there wasn't a soul in the place, no Jerries, Civvies or anyone not even a cat or a dog! The place had been practically ruined though by four months of almost continuous shelling from our positions the other side of the Rhine. When we were coming to Doorn here two days ago we came through it again and the main road now is absolutely stacked with boxes and sacks of food and fuel for miles each side of the road. The people here don't seem at all starving but we hear that further on in Amsterdam and Rotterdam the food situation is very bad. I don't think we shall be going to these places but I hope so for I should like to see them for myself.

You write such perfect descriptions of David's ways and looks and I'm sure Darling that he will grow up to be a really lovely Boy. You will be having a busy time with him now that he is getting bigger and noticing things more than before but I am glad that he is beginning to sleep through the nights and hope he continues to do so now. It did seem strange that he should sleep all night just when I came home for that week. Almost as if he knew his Mummy would be extra tired and he didn't want to worry her! What do you think Darling? The weeks simply fly by and he will be 21 weeks old tomorrow at half past two. Is he still so ravenously hungry as ever Darling. When I was at home I realized what a job you had and what a wonderful effort you made to enable yourself to supply him with sufficient milk. I don't know much about weaning but I don't suppose it will be long now before you start to feed him artificially, or am I wrong. I'm sure it must make a tremendous difference you having fed him yourself like you have because look what a wonderful Baby he is and so beautiful and contented too. Of course having such a lovely Mother as you are Darling he is bound to have been a lovely Boy and I'm sure that is mainly the reason why he is as lovable.

If I am able to let you know (and note I said 'if') when next I shall be home would you like me to let you know Darling. By that I don't mean that it is likely to be soon because it probably won't be. Anyway think it over and let me know when next you write to me. I know that half the joy of being reunited together is in the anticipation beforehand. I'm watching the days and hours tick by until it is the moment when nothing else matters except the exciting thrill of your arms around me and to hold you close to me and to kiss you again and again and hear you whisper I Love You. Darling those words mean everything to me when you say them. I get the same thrill when you confess your Love to me now as I did when those sweet words first passed your lips. It will always be an everlasting thrill because I know that ours is an everlasting Love.

Oh My Darling – how I dream of you and think of you and long for you. They are hungry dreams and yearning thoughts but patient ones because I know that you are waiting patiently for my return with an equal longing in your own heart.

And so Darling I will say Au Revoir until we meet again. Adoration is yours and yours alone and always.

Your devoted husband
and Lover
Jackxxxxx

I Love you Sweetheart and our Darling Baby with all my heart
xxxxxxxxxxxxxxxxxxxxxxxxxxxxxxxxxxxxxxxxxxxxxxxxxxxxxxxxxx
xxxxxxxxxxxxxxxxxxxxxxxxxxxxxxxxxxxxxxxxxxxxxxxxxxxxxxxxxx

> 41 High Street
> Rishton
> VE Day Night
>
> 8.5.45

My Own Beloved Jack,

And how are you spending this important day darling? At least I know you will be sitting back on your laurels and feeling thankful that the last gun has been fired.

My day has been a fairly ordinary one on the whole – apart from an extra 'cuppa' now and again and us cleaning up or washing. I dolled up in my Sunday best and took David out after Winston

waiting patiently for my return
with an equal longing in your
own Heart.

And so Darling I will
say Au Revoir until we meet
again. My Wholehearted Love
and Adoration is yours and
yours alone and always.
Your devoted Husband
and Lover
Jack. x. x x x x

I Love You Sweetheart and our
Darling Baby with all my Heart.
x x x x x x x x x Jack. x x x x x
x x x x x x x x x x x x x x x x
x x x x x x x x x x x x x x x x x x

had finished spouting and let myself imagine you were out with us and all happy together. My well worn question darling How soon will you be home again? We have the buntings out for you all the way down the road. In fact they are out specially for you I feel sure dear. I can see them now flapping about in the wind as I sit up here in bed. It's only soon after 9 pm.

They say you are disposing of thousands of prisoners or are you on that job of occupying Denmark. Whatever it is I know you will have plenty to do and far from being a holiday but its good to know that the worst is over at least where Germany is concerned.

My writing is looking all shapes tonight darling. That is because I've been giving a wart on my thumb some vigorous treatment and today I cut it off – the wart I mean – then tonight I burnt my finger on the poker which had just been in the fire for a while to make it bright. Proper old soldier I am.

Auntie Olive came round this afternoon so we wagged our tongues dry again – as usual.

Mary and Winnie came over on Sunday and Mary brought a birthday present for me – a pair of pillow slips. Very useful they will be sometime won't they darling?

The clinic was closed today being VE Day so we shall have to wait another week to know David's weight.

It is now Wednesday evening darling, usual time, usual place. Today the weather has been lovely so I have been using it to full advantage. First I did a big wash then this afternoon Mother and I took David out in the lovely sunshine.

I am waiting for a letter from you now dear for it is almost a fortnight since one came. I did hope that one would come today but it didn't, worst luck. For I do so appreciate and look forward to your letters. However who knows what tomorrow may bring.

So for now Darling Cheerio
There are hundreds of Hugs and Kisses waiting for you.

Your loving wife and son
Olive & David

LUCIA WHITEHEAD

Lucia Whitehead was brought up in London, trained as a nurse at St Mary's Paddington in 1940, and went on to become a Red Cross nurse in the Free French Convalescent Home. On 19 January 1943 she joined up, and went into the ATS Signal Platoon, before becoming PA to Brigadier Turner, deputy director of public relations with SSAEF.

Lucia's father was E. F. Lawson, then a brigadier in CRA 48th Division. After Dunkirk, Lucia's father became Director of Public Relations in the War Office until the cessation of hostilities, when he became Managing Director of the *Daily Telegraph*, which Lucia's great-great grandfather, Joseph Moses Levy, had founded. They were a close-knit family, who did everything together. Lucia learned to shoot with her brothers Bill and Hugh, and their parents would take them on trips to the zoo on fine Sundays; if it was wet, they would make toffee. 'Nothing was concealed, if we asked about something we were told. I worshipped my parents, things were always a hundred per cent honest between us, and I never remember hearing my parents argue. They seemed to be absolutely perfect. We never heard any disagreement, it's something children now don't know.'

After Lucia joined up she tried to write home once a week: 'It was an outlet because we couldn't talk to them. I wrote about everything from getting up in the morning, to going to bed at night. My parents made me what I am today. My mother was a great entertainer, permanently in the public view. She gave wonderful regimental dinner parties in the 1930s. My parents married in 1920, immediately after my father had come out of the First World War. If you'd been through that, you weren't going to waste your time having rows at home. It's awful to say it, "War brings out the best in people," but it does. Everyone was chums, everyone talked to everyone.'

In January 1940, Lucia's father wrote a 'last letter' to his wife:

My most precious,

A short letter on a very serious subject. I do not think that this war is particularly dangerous or likely to be but always remember this.

If anything happens to me it would be silly to say don't worry, but don't worry for me. I don't want to die but I am not afraid of it and I should not complain. I have had twenty years of complete and absolute happiness entirely through you, and that is perhaps as much as anyone can ask. If I get more I shall be very grateful but I have had so much that I do not feel I have any right to ask for more. I have supreme confidence in your looking after the children as I should like them to be looked after.

I am quite cheerful and as far as I myself alone am concerned face everything without fear or worry. Do be quite sure of that. I mean it and do not say it for you.

And I do love you very much – more than ever, you know that. We have had a wonderful life.

Bill of course does worry me but I would not have our son do any different [Bill Lawson, then nineteen, was serving in the Royal 99th Bucks Hussars Field Regiment, 2nd Division]. It makes a difference to one's whole future life to have played a man's part at a time like this and one must take one's chance. I think it is a very good chance indeed and trust all will be well.

I know that what I did in the last war, for what it was worth, has been the making of my whole life and has made it possible for me to enjoy the happiness that you have given me. And I will now say nothing on this subject in the future but I should not like to have gone to the war without having said it and I mean every word of it as sincerely as anything I have ever said to you.

Bless you my most precious darling and one day we will smile happily over this letter.

F

Four months later, Lucia's father wrote in similar vein, but this time facing real danger. The envelope of the letter to her mother was marked 'last letter before Dunkirk'.

My own darling,

Once again I feel compelled to write a serious letter. My only concern is for Bill and for you about us both.

Do not have the slightest worry for me for my own sake. I am extremely cheerful, not the least frightened of the prospect whatever it may be, and whatever may happen do not think I regret anything.

I have had 20 years perfect happiness and I know that if I am not lucky you will tackle the difficult future with courage. That is the only thing that matters or, as yet, to go on . . . It will be alright and we'll have a good time again sometime but we've got a bit to get through first . . .

As I said before I expect my letters will be slow now so do not think anything of that. They seem from the news to have downed a nice lot of aeroplanes which will make life more comfortable. Remember that the only thing that gives me any depression is the knowledge that you are worrying . . . My love to Lucia and to everybody . . . Write to me often as we shall be a bit short of news and somehow or other I like your letters whether there is news or not. Bless you.

Brigadier Lawson left the beaches at Lapanne. By some extraordinary chance, he and his son Bill met up on the beach at Dunkirk. According to Lucia, her father turned to Bill and uttered the words, 'You need a shave,' before anything else, and made him shave then and there, 'with his batman holding the mirror, I think!'

The Sunday of Dunkirk Lucia and her mother went to church. 'We always went to church, but that day it was stuffed with people who didn't usually go. I remember the rector leaning over the pulpit and saying, "You're frightened, you only come when you're frightened." Every prayer was addressed to get them back somehow.'

When Lucia first joined the ATS she shared a flat off Baker Street with two American girls, but, 'They caught up with me, and put me in the ATS Barracks in Gower Street, that had been the hostel for Bourne and Hollingsworth employees. The University of London was the Ministry of Information then, and that's where I worked. We were war correspondents, and we had to be in the West End, because that's where the teleprinters and telephone communications all were.'

She was there for just over six months. Then, on 11 September 1944, Lucia was taken to Paris with Brigadier Turner. It was the first time she had ever flown. For the first two months she stayed in a hotel, until, again, 'they caught up with me, and I was put in one for the lesser ranks'.

On 24 January 1945, still in Paris, Lucia wrote a letter home both to congratulate her parents on their twenty-fifth wedding anniversary, and to tell them how the war had made her realize just how much she owed them:

Supreme Headquarters
ALLIED EXPEDITIONARY FORCE
Public Relations Division

24th January 1945

Darling Mummy,

How is everything at home. My spies tell me that poor Daddy is in bed with 'flu but getting better, I hope that by the time you get this he is completely cured, 'cos I know how badly he gets it.

I have just realised that in four days the sweetest and nicest people I know in the world will have been married twenty five years and there isn't a thing I can do about it. I am scouting Paris to see if there is anyone going back to the U.K. who can send a telegram off for me, but so far without success, so if you don't receive one, it won't be for want of trying on my part. Darlings, since B.C. I don't believe two people have existed who I could have wanted more for a Father and Mother or who could have slaved more for me than you have. At times I know I may seem very ungrateful and to you it must seem that your labours have gone by unnoticed but that isn't true. I think probably the only good thing this war has done has been to make me realise how much I owe you, if you both hadn't shown me how perfect a marriage can be, my ideas on marriage, my own life, my whole outlook would have been on an entirely lower shelf and of a different standard. You were unlucky to have produced two such temperamental children as Bill and I (and possibly Hugh) but at times I wonder whether it isn't because you are both so sweet and unselfish that God thought that he couldn't make us like you as the distribution would be uneven on a world basis. Many many congratulations darling Mummy and Daddy, and may we in the next twenty five years bring you as much happiness as you have brought us in the first twenty five.

The Brigadier is away in England again, and alas he left me behind, probably through my own fault as I had last Saturday and Sunday off so as I could entertain Mr Ryan who was in Paris for three days from the 3rd U.S. Army. We had a lot of fun and a lot of heated argument owing to the fact that Corny is a R.C. and I C.of E. and somehow as was not surprising we got onto the subject of religion. I have been doing quite a bit of work for the Brigadier and I think that soon I shall be able to operate as Deputy Director of the Division with a couple of secretaries of my own.

This will not be as long a letter as usual, 'cos I want to get it off so as it gets to you as near the 28th as possible, and also I have to go out to the hospital to see one of my girls who is ill.

Bless you my twenty five years old Darlings,

Your devoted daughter,
Lucia

By the end of March, with the end of the war obviously in sight, Lucia wrote to her mother voicing her worries — worries that must have been beginning to trouble so many, at the imminence of a return to peace-time and civilian life:

27th March 1945

The news is wonderful of course, and the end of the war seems pretty near. After so many years of saying 'when the war is over' it seems almost unbelievable, and somehow I have a feeling of anti-climax, I don't know how I expected it to end, but I don't think like this, and already I am scared — what's going to happen afterwards, what is it like when there isn't a war, what is going to happen to us in the A.T.S., where will I be sent to, what will I do when I don't have to get up in the morning, don't have to dress the way I'm told, all these questions to which I can find no answer, and questions which I feel people like me are asking all over the world?

It's strange to feel lost when I know I have a home to go to, but I can't just sit at home and do nothing, at least not after about a month of it, I suppose I could take up some good 'works', or travel but neither of them appeal to me, I could get married, but I suppose I'd better find someone I love before I do that . . . This is an awful letter, but I will write again within the next few days, this was just really a note to let you know that I arrived safely and am back 'on the job'. Darling Mummy, take care of yourself, Lucia.

Lucia describes life during the war as something that completely took over. All normality was suspended: 'It was your life, you knew nothing else. I was frightened of coming home and suddenly not being told what to do. When I wrote that letter on 27 March, although I knew the war had been a very important part of my life, I felt strangely empty. You had no purpose. You were winning the war, although of course it was still going on in the Far East – regrettably that all seemed very remote from us. There wasn't anything clear to do. My father had a sense of purpose, a job to go back to, whereas anyone of our age didn't and I just didn't know what to do. I was demobilized in 1946, and married later that year to someone I'd met after I came home. It didn't last. I remember saying to my mother when I came home, "I only know how to type and scrub floors!"'

Looking back on the war, and her correspondence during it, Lucia says: 'I'd never write any of these letters now. I'd think God, you're being stupid, soppy to the nth degree, but at the time they could only have been written like that. I felt like that at the time. It was how and what you knew was going on. In many ways the war did a lot of good, produced the best possible spirit and ideals to work to which normal life didn't. It is the best and the worst of everything in life. How much love is generated by the fear of danger to another person? I think a great deal. It is a craving. The whole of everyone's emotions are permanently on a knife edge.'

Lucia's post-VE Day letter, written to her family, encapsulates the spirit of elation that swept Paris after the horrors and dangers were over:

I will try and tell you a little bit about V period over here although it is very difficult because the only thing that really describes it is to visualise thousands upon thousands of people wandering through the streets cheering, singing, laughing and kissing. Monday night was a little half hearted as no one was sure whether it was true or not but Ginny and Douglas Williams and Doug and I drove in Douglas' car up to Sacre Coeur and sat on the steps watching the aeroplanes fly over in hundreds dropping flares and as each flare dropped a big AH went up! Tuesday Ginny and I went into the office in the morning as good little girls to find no one in the building but ourselves and so we went home at about 11, having discovered that both Colonel Dupuy and the Brig had gone to Berlin to the signing of the surrender terms. We had a lunch party of about ten including Brigadier Foord and his P.A. Subaltern Gambia-Parry. At 3pm we all went up to Ginny's room to listen to the P.M. After he had spoken everything in Paris just broke loose, the sirens wailed for three minutes, the church bells rang the people cheered and shouted and hundreds of aeroplanes soared over the roof tops. We all decided that the only thing to do was to go into the streets and see the fun and so all of us wearing each others hats went down into the streets and milled along with the crowds being kissed every two minutes! After about half an hour of this we realised we were getting nowhere and so we fought our way back to the Scribe dismissed Brigadier Foord's driver and the Brigadier took over the wheel and we all climbed on the top and drove slowly amidst millions of cheering crowds down to the Place de la Concorde up the Champs Elysees until the crowds became too dense for us to move at all and then we all got out parked the car and went into the flat of a French officer who was on the top of the car with us and had a few drinks and cooled down as it was so terrifically hot. In the evening we all had dinner together and then Doug and I went to Ciro's for a while but it was too crowded and so we resorted to wandering through the streets and looking at the illuminations. All this is really impossible to describe as no one can imagine anything like the crowds there were, fourteen people were killed on the Champs Elysees and hundreds injured just from being crushed in crowds. The papers have written all this up much better than I ever could, but they didn't say how drunk everybody was in Paris, not with alcohol but with happiness!

JILL LIVOCK

Jill Livock was an airforce baby. Her father was a squadron leader in the Royal Flying Corps for eleven years before the war. He then became a group captain and later retired as an air commodore.

'There was no question of having roots anywhere. My father was often moved twice a year, we had no family home. Home was wherever my mother happened to be. I had one sister who was six years older. I was sent off to boarding school when I was eight, at Hillside Convent College in Farnborough, and stayed there till I was twelve. Then I went on to Thornton College at Bletchley in Buckinghamshire. It was a very strict routine with the nuns, we were only allowed to write home once a week on Sunday. We longed for the post, clung to it. If I didn't get a letter from my mother I was bereft, it was a link, a saviour. My mother was superb about parcels too, sending chocolate and jam, but I lived for letters. They were not very emotional, her letters. She was determined to be loyal to my father, who was very much conditioned to being stiff-upper-lipped. My father was Catholic, my mother was not.'

Jill's school was 'in the middle of nowhere', and break was the high point of the day. 'We formed a circle, and the nuns gave out the letters. I would write back longing to tell my parents what was happening. There was an incredible desire to communicate.'

VE Day, however, was the high point of Jill's school life. She wrote in her diary on 8 May 1945:

At lunch a special good one we listened to the piano, played by one of the juniors, and sung clapped and ate at the same time. And then we danced round the lunch tables ... After a good tea we played charades the different forms. At intervals we sung patriotic songs and anthems.

She remembers her diary as 'all copied from the propaganda we were getting at the time. We'd had it dinned into us that England stood alone, and we were all full of patriotic rhetoric. It was a very clever machine, the Ministry of Information. It was subtly geared to England winning:

'"Oh! how can one go on to relate what will happen again and again to many of our generations if we do not conquer hatred, brutality and all the rest of terrible human weakness? NEVER AGAIN."'

They might have been miles from anywhere, but Jill remembers looking out from school on to the world beyond celebrating VE Day, to 'searchlights triumphant in the sky. We could hear the people cheering and shouting on the radio, and we wanted to be part of it. We all managed to get hold of red, white and blue clothes, and sang patriotic songs, and played the piano and danced to all the best wartime hits.'

The impact of victory and the school's celebrations are vividly evoked in her letter home of 13 May.

May 13th

Dearest Mummy and Daddy,

Your two post-cards and your letter written last Monday arrived yesterday and I was completely overwhelmed!! I'm terribly sorry for poor Barbara and was wondering all the week what had happened to her. Poor old thing, what rotten luck to spend her leave *and* VE Day in hospital!! If only I'd known before I would have written to her but I had no idea. Please don't worry about the parcel because we are having the dance on Whit-Monday and the tuck (I hope you haven't sent anything spoilable!) I hope it will arrive tomorrow. Perhaps you would like to hear how we spent VE Day here. I did start to write to you before but didn't get very far. We were told it was VE day at breakfast but it was pretty obvious it was the night before as the seniors weren't allowed to listen in. Well we just cheered our heads off and went mad. After a hectic breakfast everybody changed into red, white and blue and I hung my flag out of the dorm window. I had my red blouse, white belt and somebody else's blue skirt on!!! After the usual Rogation day procession the school Union Jack's were put out and some of the local parents came and a few people went home. We then had a jolly good game of sardines but played quite differently from the ordinary and got ourselves thoroughly hot, tired and stung all over. Then we came in and sang all the patriotic songs with all our might and main. (At Mass after breakfast 'England' was played on the organ and I confess it was so moving I had to cry. It somehow seemed so marvellous that we had all come through. Oh! it was just unbelievable.) At lunch we sung clapped and shouted while one of the juniors played all the usual popular songs and then we got up and danced round the tables after going in the garden at 5 o'clock like the whole world must have done. We all listened in dead silence to dear old Churchill's announcement and then heard how the rest of the country was celebrating. After tea we played charades and didn't do much and sung at intervals. At 9 o'clock we listened to the King and so to bed. I know none of this sounds a bit thrilling but what *could* we do and anyway I enjoyed it. That night when everybody was asleep I watched the search lights and flares and heard the guns. I felt glad that at least half England would not sleep that night and at 1 minute past 12 (when the war officially ended) I leaned out of the window while Germany crashed. Just like that. Nations don't totter and fall every day!!!

On Wednesday we didn't do much except prepare for an impromptu entertainment given by each form and in the afternoon we had a ridiculous scavenger hunt. I was by this time fed up and bored stiff after having read how London celebrated (at present we are trying to listen to the thanksgiving service from Westminster Abbey). After the entertainment in which we all dressed up and made a fool of ourselves we again sang 'Land of Hope and Glory, England, Rule Britannia and God Save the King'. I've never sung so fervently. And so now we're just back to the usual work. Nothing but Junior Oxford drummed into us. Anyway its half term next week-end.

I'm so glad to hear the camp behaved properly. I suppose you couldn't really celebrate with poor B in hospital. How is Granny now? Please thank her very much indeed for the sweet ration. Will Daddy be having the basic petrol ration now. It would be lovely if he could come and fetch me home by car and marvellous for Mummy at home. What is going to happen to Weeton now? Will it close down and what about Daddy?

My camera is 6.20 I think. Doesn't it say. I'm awfully sorry to bother you but could you send some VE Day cuttings if you haven't all ready?? I read in the 'Daily Herald' that Churchill had driven through London in a tiny open car with his hat perched on his head and his cigar between his teeth and tears streaming down his face. This on VE night!! That I think impressed me more than anything.

I know you will show this to Barbara but I'm going to write a separate one and Tim has kindly volunteered to also!!! I do hope B is much better now. I really don't know what to say about it. How long will she be at Weeton and when do the stitches come out and how long sick leave?? *And* I hope sincerely Jim will manage her properly!!!! She's got to take notice now that Peter's out of the light. We have now got summer dresses on and the weather has been simply terrific the last two days. Tennis at last but was it hot! The dresses go to the wash 1 a fortnight and bath 1 a fortnight and cold water in the morning!!! But still we can't grumble in the least bit. How is Uncle Den getting on? Enclosed is the 6d owed since last Tuesday to Askew!! Do you like the school note-paper? 1/- for 18 sheets. Must stop now and write to Barbara. Please write very soon and thank you very much for the trouble you have taken over the coming parcel.

Best VE love and hugs
Jill

PHINEAS MAY

No _166_

BRITISH INSTITUTE
Alexandria

KK Lieut. P. L. MAY

Member, Associate Member.

Phineas May was born in 1906. Together with his brother, Jonas, who was active in the Jewish Lads Brigade, he worked at a welfare camp for Jewish refugees from Germany and Austria. Jonas was the commandant and Phineas the welfare officer. On 2 November 1941 he married his fiancée, Vivienne, and the following year, when he was thirty-five, he was commissioned as a second lieutenant. His age could have worked against him, but a family friend, Lord Reading, recommended that he be made an officer. By the end of the war he was a captain and had served in Egypt and East Africa.

During their separation, Phineas sent hundreds of cartoons home to Vivienne. After the war the complete collection was lodged with the Imperial War Museum, and with them Phineas enclosed the following piece, which describes how he beat the Army censors:

Ex-Servicemen who were on active service in the Middle or Far-East during the 1939–1945 war may recall the airgraphs which they sent as a personal communication with their loved ones.

One wrote the letter quarto size on a special sheet, which after being censored, was photographed and reduced to a tiny size and arrived measuring $3\frac{1}{2} \times 5$ inches. I used these during my three and a half years in Egypt to send cartoons which I hoped would amuse my wife and family.

After I had been sending these for some time, a Capt. 'Know-All' said they would be dangerous if they got into enemy hands and reported me to G.H.Q. Middle-East to which I was duly summoned for an interview.

Having examined specimens of my cartoons, they said they only hoped that some of them would get into enemy hands as they showed the splendid spirit of the British troops.

Vivienne remembers that all their friends wanted to see the cartoons. Phineas counters, 'I made a very good friend in the Army, and the only way I could show him what a wonderful wife I had was by showing him one of her letters. The days when the post stopped were very depressing. Her letters kept me going.'

As the Allied victory drew near, their correspondence begins to reflect

the excitement and anticipation that was in the air. Phineas wrote to
Vivienne on Sunday 15 April 1945, when the first intimations of the end
of the war had reached him in Africa:

JUST HEARD THE 1.30 NEWS . . . IT IS TERRIFIC . . . for all
intents and purposes the war in Germany is over . . . days . . .
maybe only hours . . . welcome the announcement so long awaited
. . . that it is all over . . . and it would seem that even greater news
is expected from Tokyo . . . that Japan may unconditionally
surrender at the same time . . . if that is so . . . this really will be
PEACE . . . and should mean that we should get back even quicker
and they will be able to hasten the demobbing . . . I feel terribly
excited and I am sure you are.

Three weeks later, on 6 May 1945, Phineas eagerly awaits
confirmation:

I am writing in bed having heard the wonderful news from the
B.B.C. at 10 pm that Churchill will be speaking to the world in a
day or two announcing all hostilities have ceased, and that it is VE
day . . . I hope I am with you on that momentous day.
    For so we pray it will be the start of a new era of PEACE . . .
for the world so it will see the commencement of our life together
we have looked forward to for so long . . . by the time this reaches
you I will be 39 . . . how much may happen to us both before my
40th birthday? Will we have settled down in our own home and I
in a steady job? . . . The remaining months will most probably
seem longer than the three years that has nearly gone by since we
last saw each other . . . but we must help each other over the
remaining period as we have done up to now.

On 20 May, his hope and optimism are tinged with anxiety. What
will he be coming home to? It must have been the same for so many men,
so many couples, the certainties of war, work, food, housing about to be
replaced by the uncertainties of peace, a curious paradox:

This letter is all about the very worrying question of a home. What has happened about the Government control of rents? That is a question that must be put to all M.P.'s . . . are we who have served so long to be robbed of our gratuities and savings by price racketeers? Are there going to be so many £500 a year jobs about that one can pay such exorbitant prices?

If you can get the flat in Brunswick Square do so by all means . . . we will just have to 'grin and bear' the rent for a couple of years.

By 24 July, plans for coming home were advanced, and in the meanwhile, Phineas can only imagine the joy:

I am only allowed to bring £10 with me into England in cash, but do not expect to have to spend much from the time I go abroad, to when I ring the bell at Audley Road . . . though it most probably will be best if you will leave the door ajar from an hour before you expect me so I can come straight upstairs, dump my bags in the hall, and meet you for the first time in the dining room, and we'll be causing no obstruction if we remain in each others arms for a few hours . . . say until from sheer starvation and exhaustion we stop kissing each other . . . you will have a very kiss-proof lipstick won't you – speed on that day we have so long looked forward to.

A very great heap of loving hugs and kisses. Deeply loving and devoted Phineas.

In August he wrote two last letters from his transit camp, preparing Vivienne for his arrival home, and reiterating his worries for the future, alongside his determination to make her happy in a world which 'surely we have a right to expect to live in'.

FRI 10 AUG. 1945   152 TRANSIT CAMP M.E.F.

My dearly beloved Vivienne,

Most probably this will be the last letter I will write you from the Middle East, and I hope that it will be the last that I will have to write you and that we will never experience such a long separation again.

At the moment it still seems impossible that in a few days we will be re-united again at least seven weeks earlier than we expected and avoiding that terrible drag that those weeks would have meant, and also with the glorious opportunity of spending our 4th Engagement anniversary together . . . and like so much else in my life I owe it all to you . . . we won't mention the job because I have not got it yet . . . but I think it a rather wonderful wife who not only does all she can to get her husband a position . . . but also brings him home.

I am afraid that I have been a pretty miserable correspondent the last few weeks, being very depressed with the worry of our future home and how I could best pick an occupation to support you in the way you so richly deserve, added to that I have been continually threatened with compulsory deferment on the Military Vital Clause, and only on Tuesday morning I was told I had not a hope in returning in September. But all is well that ends well.

It is no good at that stage making you all sorts of promises which look very beautiful in words, but are not easy to carry out. But I only hope that I will not be disappointed in my dreams for your happiness in the near future. I have so much to make up for, I owe you so much in so many ways and up to now it is you who have given me so much in happiness and help in so many ways . . . and what have I done . . . nothing . . . but occasionally moan over my fate.

Happiness is a very illusive thing, sometimes it seems so near, and yet just as you think you have caught hold of it, it slips out of your fingers like a butterfly.

Anyway, with you constantly at my side, I hope you will never fail to remind me if you feel that life is becoming dull and not altogether happy for you.

I know you are not a person who likes to make a set plan for the future, but I have a few ideas which I will discuss with you on my return which I hope will add to a life, that otherwise just keeping a home for me will seem dull after the first novelty has worn off.

At the moment I have not the foggiest idea what leave I will get on my return to England but I will be notified as soon as I arrive . . . normally you get a week for every years service overseas . . . and if they do that, well that would bring me to the beginning of Sept. and it would hardly seem worthwhile their posting me for the remaining 24 days before my release . . . but we shall see.

It is all very exciting and it is curious to think what I or we, may be doing when this letter arrives . . . though it is possible it will reach you first . . .

In case it does . . .

I will give you once more a very unsatisfactory written hugs and kisses, and pray it will be the last time that I give Sabbath Greetings this way.

Deeply loving and very devoted,
Phineas

FRI 10 AUG. 1945   CAPT. MAY
2nd Letter   152 TRANSIT CAMP M.E.F.

My dearly beloved Vivienne,

It is 4.20 and it has just been announced that Japan has uncon-ditionally surrendered, and that we pray will be the last of War in my lifetime . . . and what a wonderful moment for the Chinese peoples who have been wearied of war so long it was obvious that one nation however devilish or cunning could not long resist a whole world, and if it lasted long enough to demonstrate what horror awaits those who start another war, they will have been two vital months in the history of the world.

For most people it has been so distant . . . distant even from here . . . That like myself they have talked about the 'lights going on again all over the world' . . . but now they will . . . and now all the vast factories turning out weapons of destruction can be turned very soon to the much needed articles of domestic life.

Of course this really is peace . . . but it will seem an after-climax having so recently celebrated V.E. day. I hope that we can celebrate this real Victory day together. Of course I am not forgetting that for years and years to come . . . there is going to be ghastly suffering as a result of the terrible conflict just finished . . . but it does mean that from these days I am about to return to you, each day it will be a step nearer the world surely we have a right to expect to live in.

It is certainly proving a remarkable week, and not one that we are ever likely to forget . . . though I earnestly pray that nothing will prevent next week being an even greater one in our lives.

A World of love my angel on this great day.

Ever most deeply loving and devoted and with extra loving hugs and kisses for this great day.

Phineas

Phineas and Vivienne have now been together for fifty-four years. On his return they had a daughter and a son and they live in North London.

EPILOGUE

The VE Day celebrations, wonderful though they were, did not signal the end of the war, or the end of many people's life of separation and letter-writing. Indeed, the whole process of demobbing and completing commissions meant that men were still returning as late as 1947 and 1948.

What VE Day did, in a curious sense, was to represent the beginning of a new era, much as had the outbreak of war. Young men and women had grown up through their wartime experiences and this was reflected in their correspondence.

VE Day was another turning point. The fear with which so many had lived had been replaced by hope. That hope, even when tempered by doubt and uncertainty, signalled a new chapter for those still separated both physically and emotionally in every sense but for their letters.

How much love is generated by the fear of danger to another person? I think a great deal. It is a craving. The whole of everyone's emotions are permanently on a knife edge.

Lucia Whitehead, looking back from a perspective of fifty years, captured perfectly the extraordinary intensity that became a part of everyday life during the war.

If the letters in this book have one thing in common, it is that they all reflect that intensity, and, more importantly, the love that had been the inspiration behind the letter-writing in the first place.